A BRAVE Journey

Thoughts on Reclaiming Your Identity in Mid-Life

by Sharon Welch

1

A BRAVE Journey: Thoughts on Reclaiming Your Identity in Mid-Life
Copyright © 2026 by Sharon Welch, She Live Out Loud
All rights reserved.

Disclaimer

This book is intended for informational and inspirational purposes only. The author is not a licensed medical, mental health, financial, or legal professional, and the content of this book does not constitute professional advice or services. Always seek the advice of qualified professionals regarding any questions you may have about your physical or mental health, finances, legal matters, or any other topic requiring expert guidance. The reader assumes full responsibility for how they choose to use the information contained in this book. The author and publisher disclaim any liability for any loss, injury, or damage incurred as a consequence, directly or indirectly, of the use and application of any content within this book.

Personal Transformation & Emotional Safety Notice

This book includes themes related to identity, personal transformation, relationships, belonging, emotional healing, and self-reflection. Some content may be emotionally activating. Please care for yourself gently as you read, and consider pausing or seeking support if you feel overwhelmed.

Names and Identifying Details

Some names, identifying details, timelines, and situations have been changed to protect the privacy of individuals. Any resemblance to actual persons—living or dead—is coincidental.

Trademarks

Any references to trademarks, brands, organizations, or products are made for informational purposes only. All trademarks are the property of their respective owners.

Published by: The Live Out Loud Press

First Edition: February 2026
ISBN: 979-8-218-91179-9

Cover design: Arcane Book Design

Printed in the United States of America

Thank you for supporting independent authors and brave conversations.

To my soul family —

the beautiful humans who walked with me through the unraveling and the rising,

the ones who chose me,

held me,

mirrored my truth,

and reminded me who I was becoming

long before I could see it myself,

and who showed me what true belonging feels like.

Thank you for being my safe harbor,

my teachers,

my mirrors,

and my home.

This book carries your fingerprints.

Table of Contents

The She Lives Out Loud Manifesto   **6**

Welcome Home   8

So, Who the Heck Am I?   13

Waypoint One – The Awakening   **23**

    Is This You?   24

    The Ache Beneath "Fine"   30

    The Non-Story IS The Story   32

    The First Whispers of Restlessness   35

    Why It's Important to Tell My Story Now   37

    When the Universe Whispered Back   40

Waypoint Two – The Unraveling   **43**

    When Strong Stops Working   44

    About Being Brave   46

    Transforming Through Life's Curveballs   50

    Adventures and Gaslighting at
the Bottom of The World   56

    The Cost of Holding it all Together   63

    The Mirror and the Reckoning   65

Waypoint Three – The Reckoning   **67**

    What is an Identity Anyway?   68

    Conforming for Comfort   76

    The Vulnerability Paradox   82

Waypoint Four – The Reclamation   **87**

     The Unintended Consequences of Facades   88

     Feeling the Weight   92

     The Seduction of Comfort   95

     Meaning or Purpose?   101

Waypoint Five – The Integration   **107**

     Don't Make it Special   108

     Rest is the Secret Sauce   111

     Reintegrating the Extraordinary into the Typical   116

     The Now and the Not Yet   122

Waypoint Six – The Expansion   **131**

     We Are All the Same   132

     Happiness Does Not Exist (Out There)   135

     Curious About Curiosity   141

     Connection and Community   149

     The Loneliness Factor   155

The Spark   **162**

About the Author   163

She Lives Out Loud Manifesto

We are the women who woke up one morning and couldn't pretend anymore.

We checked all the boxes, followed all the rules, and smiled on cue —

only to find ourselves empty, restless, and wondering, "Is this all there is?"

But beneath the layers of "should" and "supposed to,"

our souls were whispering — and then shouting — No more.

No more shrinking to fit.

No more silencing our truth to make others comfortable.

No more apologizing for wanting more —

more joy, more depth, more meaning, more of ourselves.

We are the women who have walked through lifequakes,

who have watched our carefully built worlds crumble —

and instead of burying the pieces,

we picked them up and built something truer.

We are the seekers and the questioners,

the travelers and the truth-speakers,

the connectors, creators, and quiet revolutionaries.

We are not waiting for permission anymore.

We are writing new rules — our own.

We lead with courage,

live with vulnerability,

love with abandon,

and rise — together.

Because when one woman chooses to live out loud,

she doesn't just change her life.

She changes the lives of everyone who sees her.

This is not a rebellion born of anger,

but a reclamation born of love.

Love for ourselves,

love for one another,

love for this world that needs us whole and awake.

We are the bridge between what was and what's next —

between breakdown and breakthrough,

between fear and freedom,

between the illusion of control and the truth of connection.

We are living out loud.

And we are just getting started.

Welcome Home

A BRAVE Journey

"Belonging shouldn't cost you your truth."

There's a moment- quiet, inconvenient, and impossible to ignore—when you realize you've been living inside a life that looks fine... but doesn't feel like you.

Maybe it happens in the mirror, when your eyes meet your own and something in you flinches. Maybe it happens in the middle of a meeting, when you hear yourself speak and think, Who is that? Maybe it happens in bed at night, when the world finally goes quiet enough for your truth to start knocking. You don't always know how to explain it. You just know something is off.

You've built the life you were supposed to build. You've hit the milestones. You've held it together. You've succeeded— at least by the standards that were handed to you. And yet... a part of you has been quietly negotiating with the question:

Is this all there is?

Or worse:

Is this really who I am?

I wrote this book for that moment.

Not the moment when everything is falling apart—although it can feel that way. But the moment when everything looks fine... and you're still hungry.

Hungry for truth.
Hungry for ease.
Hungry for connection that doesn't require performance.

Hungry for a version of yourself that doesn't need to be edited, managed, diluted, or muted to be loved.

A version of you that feels like you again.

What This Book Is

A BRAVE Journey is a collection of essays, reflections, and lived moments— some subtle, some seismic— written for the woman who is waking up.

Waking up to the ways she has conformed for comfort. Waking up to the belief systems she inherited and never questioned. Waking up to the ways she has abandoned herself— not because she was weak, but because she was surviving.

This is not a "10 steps to fix your life" book.

It's not a productivity manual, a mindset checklist, or a perfect blueprint.

It's a companion.

A mirror.
A deep exhale.
A truth-telling conversation with yourself.

This is the book I wish someone had handed me back when I was strong on the outside... and quietly disappearing on the inside.

What This Book Is Not

Let me say this clearly:

This is not a book about burning your life down. It's not about becoming someone completely different. It's not about chasing some glossy "best version of yourself" that sounds suspiciously like another performance.

This is about returning.

Returning to the parts of yourself you buried in order to belong. Returning to the instincts you overruled to be liked. Returning to the voice you softened so you wouldn't make waves. Returning to your body—because your body has been trying to tell you the truth the whole time.

And yes… returning to your aliveness.

Why BRAVE?

Because at some point, you realize this journey requires something more than insight. More than intention. More than another book you highlight and then forget.

This journey requires courage. And not the dramatic kind. Not the bold-move, jump-off-a-cliff kind. The everyday kind. The kind that looks like:

— telling the truth in a room where you used to stay quiet
— taking off the mask even when you're not sure what's underneath yet
— admitting you don't know what you want… and staying open anyway
— choosing rest when your old identity demands productivity
— letting yourself be seen
— letting yourself change

That is why this book is built around the B.R.A.V.E. framework:

Bold.
Resilient.
Authentic.
Vulnerable.
Evolving.

You don't need to become B.R.A.V.E. You already are. This book is simply here to remind you.

The Invisible Cost of "Fine"

One of the most surprising realizations I had on my own journey is that the hardest part wasn't failing. The hardest part was succeeding in a life that required me to betray myself. When you're succeeding, people celebrate you. They reward you. They admire you. And that makes it harder to admit the truth:

The version of you they love might not be the real you.

So you keep going.

You keep refining the performance.
You keep tightening the mask.
You keep conforming— because it works.

Until it doesn't.

Until you reach that breaking point where the discomfort of staying the same becomes louder than the fear of changing. And then you find yourself standing in the in-between... what I call the space between the now and the not yet. That awkward, liminal space where you are no longer who you were... but you're not quite sure who you are becoming.

This book is for that space.

How to Read This Book

You can read these essays straight through, like a journey. Or you can read them like medicine: opening to the page you need most today. Some chapters may feel like an exhale. Others may feel like a mirror you weren't expecting.

That's okay.

Take what resonates. Let what doesn't... move on. Read slowly. Stop when you need to. Come back when you're ready. There is no finish line here. There is no perfect version of transformation.

This is a journey of remembering. A journey of shedding. A journey of becoming. And it doesn't happen all at once. It happens in small brave moments. In honest breaths. In quiet choices.

A Promise

Here is what I can promise you:

You are not alone.

Not in your questions.
Not in your fear.
Not in your longing.
Not in your grief for who you used to be.

You're not broken. You're waking up. And what feels like discomfort… is often the doorway to freedom.

So if you're standing at the threshold— if you feel like you're on the edge of something but you don't know what…

Welcome.

You're exactly where you're meant to be.

Take a deep breath.

And let's begin.

A BRAVE Breath

"You don't have to betray yourself to belong."

So, Who the Heck am I?

"The question isn't who you were — it's who you are now."

My name is Sharon. I am a mother, a daughter, a sister, and a friend. I am adopted, an entrepreneur, business owner, a consultant, a corporate strategist, a Realtor and a program manager. I am a leader, a coach, a mentor, and a guide. I am a bookworm, a personal growth fanatic, a lifelong learner. I am a singer, a hiker, and a volunteer in my community. I am a supporter of veterans' reintegration, community mental health, and food desert awareness. I am a curious citizen of the world. A connector, community builder and aliveness activist.

I am resilient, self-aware, creative, charismatic, grounded, a dreamer, a planner, healthy and vibrant, high energy, an extroverted introvert, a force of nature, a natural leader.

Today, I write, travel, speak, and support super women all over the world who are stuck and exhausted. My mission is to show them how they can ditch the facade, keep their power, love their life, and most importantly feel alive again.

But it wasn't always this way. There were years in my life where I too had felt disconnected from myself, exhausted, and stuck. There was a time where I had forgotten who Sharon really was.

How many of you are feeling disconnected from who you are right now? How many of you are forcing yourself to live by an imaginary checklist of things that supposedly defines your worth, credibility and acceptability? This was me, just a few years ago.

I lived in accordance with a set of rules, following an imaginary checklist that someone, maybe my parents, society, community, handed to me— a list of things I had to do in order to be liked and accepted. When I didn't check these things off the list, I felt as though

13

I wasn't enough. So, I numbed myself and just went through it. I was curating my Facebook with glamorous jobs and exotic trips just to hide what was going on inside. But the truth was that it didn't feel so glamorous inside. It didn't matter how tired I was. I never stopped asking myself if I really wanted it. I just went through the list and was checking items off that would make me feel worthy.

How many times have we wanted to show the outside world that everything is okay but, on the inside, we were absolutely not okay? I was doing a great job hiding my hot mess and ignoring the storm brewing. That is until a series of lifequakes came, shook up my entire life, and I could no longer hide behind the facades I had created to cope with my inauthentic life.

A lifequake is an event that takes everything that you've built and shakes it all up. I watched my entire life and everything that I had built come crashing down all at once. It was during these lifequakes that I realized what I had been building wasn't real — like a house of cards, it was flimsy and unstable.

Lifequake number one was losing my job of 14 years due to a combination of the economy, internal corporate challenges, and being the target of a sociopath who cut my self-worth, sanity, and resilience down to rubble. I was nothing, or at least I definitely felt that way.

Lifequakes can also bring aftershocks, and these surprising tremors can be the most painful and eye-opening. How many of you are bracing for your own lifequake right now?

Then by trying to focus on myself to heal from losing my job, my marriage fell apart. Since I could not be the nurturer, healer, builder, and caretaker to my husband, I stopped being the person that my husband had become conditioned to expect. I was standing on top of more rubble.

Then, yet another lifequake came but this one was massive and global. Hello, pandemic!

Everything I had based my life and identity on was now either in flames, ripped out from under me, or otherwise gone forever. I had no internally based compass or definition for who I was anymore. I had been defined by my career, my relationships, my accomplishments and awards, my education, my place in the world and how I compared to everyone else for most of my adult life. Now after all of these lifequakes, all of that was largely meaningless.

As the world was shutting down around me, I was asking myself, who was Sharon? By my old definition, I was exactly nobody. I was coming apart and left exposed. So, with nothing left to lose, the universe forced me into a full reset. What do you do after coming undone, falling apart and feeling exposed? For me, I needed to leave. I wanted some space from the rubble.

I packed up some clothes and a few belongings that meant something to me and left the rest behind with my ex-husband. I drove nine hours to Cape Cod from D.C through state border checks and deserted roadways. It was just me and a few cars on the road during a global shut down. I was on my way to peace, a beautiful 300 sq ft cottage owned by my cousin. It truly felt like the end of the world, my world.

This cottage became my home and refuge for the next six months. During this time alone, I made some realizations. One of the things that I realized is that when you're going through it and the whole world looks like it is on fire, it is only when you come out of that fog do you realize it was just the glasses that you were wearing. When you feel like the world is on fire, it is really impossible to NOT see the world on fire. There is almost no way to slip a note from your future self to say, "trust me, there is another side."

Another realization I had during my time alone was that change is the only constant. It is really difficult to tell yourself that because humans don't have these tools. We want to believe that we are truly in control, even though we are never fully in control. There comes a point in our lives where we get sick of our own BS and will need to take the glasses off.

I had finally just had enough. It was intolerable for me to float around the earth with no direction and no identity. So, I allowed myself to get mad. And in that rage, I started saying yes to things just to see what I actually wanted, liked, or thought I needed. From the rubble came this newfound fiery energy, and for the first time, I was choosing me. As bad as things were, who I was, the Sharon of the past, present, and future was not going to tolerate this shit show.

So, I came out of the wallowing. There were no more tears to cry. There was no more Ben and Jerry's to eat. All the clothes got put in the laundry. Don't be afraid of it. Sometimes, the lifequakes come through our lives and it seems like the end of the world as we know it— and then inexplicably, surprisingly, gratefully— there's sunshine. Sometimes, it's actually a good thing that everything went to crap. Because it is in those moments of near emotional and spiritual dying, between despair and discomfort, I wanted more than anything to just feel alive again. Only when we are faced with our potential death do we reconnect with our aliveness and our desire to live a life that we truly love. I was telling myself, "There has got to be one more in you." One more time, Sharon. Get angry, Sharon. You have to do something. You have to.

We go through what we go through and then we have a choice to make. What they don't tell you about the infamous breakdown before the breakthrough is that there is ALWAYS a breakdown before a breakthrough. It's understanding that when you're at that point of being completely broken down, that it isn't just a death to an old life, but a rebirth of a new beginning.

If you can always recognize that there is a breakdown before that breakthrough, then you'll know there's only just one more hill to go over. After that hill, you'll realize that life is going to happen whether you participate or not. So, you decide— are you going to let it happen

16

TO you or FOR you? For women like me, like us, I don't think our egos would let us give up, do more of the same, or do nothing for too long. Something needed to change. I needed to change.

So, I got up. I started saying yes to anything and everything that piqued my interest. I signed up for an international teaching certification course so that I would be ready to teach and travel overseas If I wanted to. I started training to get my real estate license, because I thought it would be interesting to help my cousin and her real estate business. I took several certification courses in disaster response through FEMA because it nourished my soul to be able to deploy with my favorite non-profit group. I was excited that I had a plan and felt confident about my future. If you aren't saying "Yes!" to yourself— then who is?

Now, I was just waiting for the pandemic to end so that I can turn my plans into aligned action. As we all know, the pandemic didn't end in just a few months of March 2020. So, I had to pivot again. I was going to miss the hiring season for teaching English abroad. Pivot. The cottage that I was staying in was going to shut down for the winter and I was going to need a new home. Pivot.

I was hitting roadblocks, but I didn't want to turn around and go back to the life I knew. All this forward motion had to go somewhere. So, I decided to choose the path of least resistance. I went where the energy easily flowed. And again, for women like me, deciding to let go of control in this way is a huge change. I didn't understand it, but I knew I had to trust it. The glasses came off and I realized that the world around me WASN'T on fire. But I also realized that it wasn't exactly the same world that I had known either.

When we decide to rebuild our lives after a massive lifequake, we don't go back to the life we knew. During the healing process, we find power in our imagination to create a new and better world for our future self. After a massive lifequake, we reach for our aliveness and reconnect with the things that truly give us life.

I left Cape Cod and moved out west to sunny southern California near the beautiful ocean where I knew my soul would feel the most at home, free, and happy. I was offered a position back at my old company and I accepted the offer with a fresh perspective. This time, instead of breaking out of the facade, I was choosing to reenter it with full self-love and awareness that this would be my temporary solution until I figured out my next steps. I invested in myself— for the first time in a long time. I started being vulnerable— sharing my story— expanding my tribe. I have even recently fulfilled the dream of buying an investment property overseas. Following my dreams and investing in myself has become my vocation!

When I got back to my corporate job, I looked around and wondered, "How did I do this for almost 14 years?". It confirmed the change that I wanted and needed to make. So, I kept moving forward. Through my own transformational journey, I sharpened my coaching skills, I nurtured a community of friends, and I found my natural and authentic rhythm. I let the facades I had dragged with me for years fall away— never to return. Reconnecting to your aliveness is the first step to finding your authentic self— and the life you were meant to live.

The funny thing about breaking through the facade is that once you see it, you can't unsee it. And the beautiful thing about being aware of where the facades exist in our lives is that once we acknowledge the space between what society expects of us and what we expect of ourselves, we can choose how we want to stand in that spot. We can choose how powerful we want to be. We can choose how much space we want to occupy. The facade doesn't have power over me, nor you.

Today, I feel completely alive because those facades don't have power over me. I look back now at the last few years, and I find that I am a completely new species. I have lost more than 60 pounds. I am more active than ever. I have found hobbies for myself that I enjoy and make time for. I travel more – both by myself and with others. I have a circle of close friends who I cherish. I have a new love interest who is all the things I didn't know how to ask for. I am pursuing my calling in life to guide and support other super women on their own transformational journeys. I am more happy, confident and more centered than I have ever been.

When we are committed to the journey and not the outcome, we allow ourselves to receive unexpected opportunities. We don't know what we don't know, that's exactly why we don't know it. If we grip too tightly to our version of the end game, we may miss an entire universe of alternate (and even better) outcomes. How many times are we going to keep denying ourselves of our own aliveness? Of the possibilities of even better and happier outcomes?

I can tell you; I lived a large portion of my adult life behind the mask of the woman who had all her shit together, who always knew what to do, who always had the answers, who always seemed to make things work. It felt like that was what I was supposed to do – and that belief had so much inertia that it continued to build into a pretty unmanageable mountain of stress and fear of being found out. But I always thought that by attempting to show up as what everyone else wanted and expected of me was the way I could best support the people I love. Turns out, that's not true.

By denying my authentic self and being someone I was not, I was depriving others of my gifts, my deep and meaningful support, my authentic love – and most of all, I was setting a false bar or standard in my world that others would try to emulate so they could be more like me. I was selling a false bill of goods – that nobody could live up to – I was actually setting those I loved up for failure. (I have a story about that I will share later!)

Truly loving yourself is the first step to basically everything else. When you decide you love and appreciate your mind, your body, your heart, your intelligence – without rules or checklists – you become so much more available to truly interact with the world in a powerful way. My question to the superwoman reading this, do you love and appreciate who you are at this moment? And if the answer is not yet, or not fully, what is one small thing you can do today that makes you happy?

I am sharing my story with you because I want you to know who you are, and I want you to truly feel alive. Simple as that. I don't want you to have to experience a lifequake for you to start thinking about what will make you happy. Although for some of you, you might need to go through that process and that's okay too.

I want to tell you now that if you're a super woman who is tired, exhausted, or thinking of breaking the facade, that you deserve to have a life that you shouldn't have to settle for. You deserve a life where you get to be your true self. A life where you get to have what you want and need. This is all possible.

As I look back on my life, I see so many glimpses of my true self that had wanted to shine through before I shrouded them to fit into a narrative that I thought I needed to play out. So many missed opportunities to get to the good stuff faster! It is both painful and inspiring to think back through my history where I unearthed or remembered those glimmers.

Everybody deserves a life where we just want to pinch ourselves at all the goodness that pops up for us every day – the love, the energy, the money, the connection, the joy, the vitality, the deep satisfaction in doing our soul's work. All of it. Everybody deserves that, especially you.

Don't wait for a lifequake to come shake things up, start with getting off autopilot. Be your own force of nature. Start by asking yourself, what is one small thing you can do today that will connect you with your sense of aliveness?

A BRAVE Breath

You are not here to perform who you are —
you are here to remember her.

WAYPOINT ONE — THE AWAKENING

Where the ache becomes a truth you can no longer unhear.

The Awakening is the moment you first recognize that something is off. It's the whisper that interrupts your carefully constructed life and says: "This isn't right. This isn't me. There has to be more than this." It's subtle at first— a feeling you can't quite name, a restlessness you try to ignore, a question that won't stop asking itself. You might not even realize you're in an awakening until you look back and see that this was the moment everything started to shift.

Is This You?

"If you've been saying you're fine, but your soul knows you're not...
this is for you."

That lack of energy you are feeling? That disgust you feel when you look in the mirror? That frustration you are feeling because your career, your relationship . . . .your life . . .feels stuck and uncomfortable? Yeah, it's there for a reason— and it's not going away....Unless you change your mind. Change the story you are telling yourself about it.

So, hey Super Woman! Yep, you right there . . .you *can* ditch those heavy, exhausting facades you are lugging around and claim your aliveness superpower— making your own rules and living as authentically   YOU!

You see, you carry hundreds if not thousands of stories about yourself in your subconscious. And you tell these stories to yourself every day. You know them by heart. And they are serving a purpose. A purpose you invented. To be loved. To feel safe. To fit in. To be acceptable. Or...to be UN-deserving. To be IN-visible. To be what everyone else said you were supposed to be— or to be NOTHING like they wanted.

They are YOUR stories— so natural to you that you don't even really see them anymore. But trust me, they are there. Quietly holding you to the conditions and rules you set up for yourself (or the rules you let someone else set up for you that you never questioned.)

The great thing about our minds is that they come fully equipped with all kinds of cool features- like a luxury car. This means they can be controlled and conditioned in whatever manner we wish— the power of thought so to speak, depending on the situation.

24

The auto pilot features are very helpful in managing the thousands of thoughts and processes it takes for our human body to get through a day alive. Our mind is a high-performance machine that always does a great job at getting us to exactly where we set the GPS to, all the while ensuring all our systems are functioning together to keep us alive.

But what about that GPS? When was the last time you checked where it was set to take you? Have you ever? Or are you basically sitting in the back of a random Uber with no idea of the destination…just wondering grumpily to yourself why you don't recognize the roads— don't see your house- can't get to any of the interesting stops on your wish list.

Sometimes you need to shift out of autopilot to take a look at that GPS and where it is programmed to go. You may need to stop the current route and put in a new one. One that YOU decide. One that YOU want. Once you have done the work and followed the process to reprogram your GPS, you can then allow auto pilot to return to assist you again. Because now all the automatic things are happening to support your OWN vision and desires. Like magic.

Step one for you may be to get rid of the most common limiting beliefs that are holding you back – it's low hanging fruit! This primes the pump for you to find even more of those hidden stories you are telling yourself.

Think about this quote from The Scarlet Letter "She had not known the weight, until she felt the freedom . . ." Wow, did this one hit me hard! Have you ever had that experience? You had been living or acting a certain way— or tolerating some kind of behavior or experience— and you didn't even recognize the weight of it until you were on the other side of it?

This happens to all of us. We carry around these heavy and exhausting expectations created by others about who we are supposed to be and how we are supposed to act. We go along to get along. We think that this is "just the way it is." We do this so often and for so long, that we

25

become completely numb or blind to the toll of that. We normalize it. This is the fallout of living on auto pilot. It's only when we actively engage in our lives and advocate for ourselves, our needs and desires that we can shed that crushing weight.

Think about the times you have experienced the toll of carrying around the weight of others expectations and judgement the next time you are tempted to do so. Remember what it felt like— what you had to do to recover. Keep those experiences and feelings in your active memory so you can more quickly shift out of that dangerous autopilot the next time. How much of the weight of other people's expectations and definitions of what is acceptable have you been carrying around? When will you decide to put all that down once and for all?

The great news is, this is a muscle you can build over time. Soon, you will have a finely tuned radar that detects the toxicity with laser accuracy so you can stay on your path of authenticity in a life you have the freedom to be madly in love with!

I've been there. You *ARE* a super woman— and everyone knows it. In fact, they *expect* it. And that's really part of the problem. Once you have set that bar, and everyone expects you to have all your stuff together, have all the answers, lead the charge . . .it can feel exhausting, intimidating, even inauthentic at times.

Please hear this— it is OK not to have everything perfectly together ALL the time. It is OK to not always have the answers. It is OK to sometimes need the kind of support and guidance you give to everyone else. None of these things make you ANY LESS of a rock star than you are. I PROMISE! In fact, recognizing when you need support— recognizing your own blind spots— being vulnerable enough to ask for help . . .these are the things that make you even MORE powerful in your own life and in the lives of those you are impacting every day.

Showing up B.R.A.V.E. means you are being Bold. Resilient. Authentic. Vulnerable. Evolving. True "Super Women" are doing this every day— and its how those in their lives find the inspiration and permission to do the same. Don't get in your own way. Your people need you. Be willing to get what you need to be fully who you are.

You played the game, followed the rules, and put everyone else in front of yourself... and then numbed out on autopilot just to get through it all – am I right? And you STILL got kicked in the teeth, left empty-handed, without the promised prize in the box. Right again? Well, screw that! Those rules? That game? Those expectations of others? They are completely made up by someone who didn't ask YOUR opinion – and they just don't actually apply (or work!) to get you what you really want and deserve.

Does any of THIS sound familiar? You can't quite find the magic formula that works for your specific body to maintain a healthy body weight, combat the compulsion of emotional eating, manage and reduce your stress level, or maintain the level of energy you require to live your life fully and joyfully. You are challenged by attracting and managing the level of financial resources required to experience the personal freedom you desire. You hesitate to ask for and receive what you want or need, or even to allow yourself to deserve or have the permission to feel fulfilled and aligned authentically to your purpose. You resist falling in love with yourself because of a list of "shoulds" that you never seem to live up to. You settle for an "ok" life because it is easy and safe – but feel "the niggle" every day asking you why there isn't more. You feel disconnected from loved ones, community . . .yourself – and avoid navigating "unsafe" concepts of trust, surrender and vulnerability.

You are in the right place if You feel squished into a life that no longer fits or suits you. You are tired of trying to live up to the rules and standards the outside world seems to judge you by. You have dreams and goals inside you that make you giddy, but you hide them away because you don't think they are possible, or you don't deserve them. You feel alone or misunderstood and crave finding someone who "gets it!" You have a sense that something is out of alignment or just plain not working in your current life state.

27

You want more or different but have no idea how to move towards it – or worse yet, aren't even sure you're "allowed" to do things differently. You have an idea or inkling that you're not living authentically – or are just going through the motions – and the dividends have become less and less satisfying. You find yourself wondering if this is all there is – if perhaps settling for mediocre is what happens to everyone. You have always felt that you needed to HAVE more (degrees, experience, money, physical characteristics, etc.) to BE who you want to be.

You are angry that being the "good" or "dutiful" or even "masculine" woman didn't have the payoff that was promised.

You are not broken. You do not need to be fixed. You have all the wisdom you need already inside you to be your best self, and to live the life you desire. You need space held for you to really access that intuition to start benefiting from it. You need clarity about how you want to show up in the world and how to take the intentional steps to get there. You need to build a system with the right support and accountability that sets you up for inevitable success.

You may have tried to change a habit or behavior in the past only to find that your results were short lived. Many people find that once the willpower or work ethic or the reward system loses steam, they revert back to old patterns – frustrated and feeling like they failed. Does that sound familiar?

This is because focusing on the habit or behavior itself is only scratching the surface – it only addresses a symptom, not the root cause. Our habits and behaviors are the external manifestation of the belief system we hold – the belief system that forms our identity. Many of us have belief systems we inherited from our parents or other caregivers, and it has been reinforced for many years by the environment we live in. Most of us have never paused to reexamine that belief system to confirm if it still makes sense to us or serves our highest selves. It is this "changing your mind" that is the secret superpower of meaningful and permanent habit change. You have had this power all along. It is just waiting for you to reclaim it. There is a better way! When you can change your mind, you change your life.

A BRAVE Breath

"If your life looks fine but feels hollow, your truth is trying to find you."

The Ache Beneath "Fine"

"Fine is the softest prison — and the hardest one to notice."

"How are you?"
"Fine."

"Fine" is such a common response to "How are you?" And also can be so dangerous.

Fine is a universal script— safe, tidy, socially acceptable.
But fine is also dangerous.
Fine is almost never the truth.
Fine is a compromise, a cop-out.
Fine is a mask.

Fine is the version of ourselves we offer the world when the full truth feels too heavy, too complicated, or too vulnerable to speak aloud.

I lived "fine" for years.
Fine was shorthand for mild dissatisfaction, for quiet ache, for longing I didn't yet have words for.
Fine was a way to disappear inside a version of my life that looked successful but felt misaligned.

What I didn't see then— what so many women don't see— is that "fine" is often the first sign that something deeper is stirring.
The ache beneath "fine" is the beginning of awakening.

For as long as I can remember, I was a shower-crier.
In the world, I held everything together— calm, steady, capable. The one who soothed others, the fixer, the dependable one.
But behind closed doors, under the sound of running water, I would crumble.

And not gentle tears.
The kind of ugly, convulsing sobs that shake you loose from yourself.

The kind where you slide down the tile wall, collapsing into the corner, letting the water wash away the evidence of your breaking.

Then I'd stand up, towel off, and step back into the world as if nothing had happened.

I didn't know it then, but those shower-floor moments were not weakness.
They were whispers.
Signals.
Small ruptures in a life that was trying to hold too much, too tightly, for too long.

It would take years before I understood that the ache beneath "fine" wasn't a failure— it was an invitation.

A BRAVE Breath

"Let the small truths rise. They're not interruptions — they're invitations."

The Non-Story IS the Story

"Unremarkable is what is remarkable"

You know, I have lived most of my life like most women. I have had jobs. I've had a family and friends. I've worked in my community. I did the things that I was supposed to do, tried to do as many things as I could think of that I wanted to do, and have led (in my mind) a fairly unremarkable life. Sure, I've had challenges. I've even had events in my life that felt like the absolute end of the world. But let's get real. Everybody has that in their lives. It's nothing special— nothing to write home about, so to speak.

I have seen so many "hero journey" stories. These are people who suffered dramatic circumstances or events that feel so monumental that literally a movie could be made from them. These people also seem to have that one sparkly moment or turning point that they can point to as where the big win or the transformation started. I don't have all that dramatic of a story. I have a typical and even average life in many ways. I have not been physically brutalized. I have not been overtly discriminated against. I have not been homeless or penniless. I have not battled a severe and debilitating illness or physical trauma.

I don't have that one defining circumstance or realization to point to as the beacon of light for others to be inspired by. I just don't. So for this reason, I have resisted the idea that I can turn my life journey into something like the examples I keep being given for how to create that hero's journey with the powerful story arc. It just ends up feeling intimidating, inauthentic and basically impossible.

So, as I started to do this work with women, helping them to reexamine and curate their own life stories, how to change mindsets come up with different ways to lead more fully abundant, fulfilling and authentic lives, I struggled with it. How do I relate? How can I be the Pied Piper of middle of the road, mildly dissatisfied women everywhere? I really struggled with it. And then one morning while I was doing my very best to attempt to quiet my mind and meditate (and I do say attempt because I struggle with it), there was something that came from inside me as a quiet voice that said, "the unremarkable story is the story."

The fact that my life is exactly the life that millions of other women live out just like me is exactly the point. Most people don't have a Lifetime Network original movie worthy life. So we think that what we have is fine. It's ok. It's all there is. We are not in crisis. What we have must be what we should have. We see the stories about the people who overcome dramatic and seemingly insurmountable odds to win at life. And while we are inspired and buoyed by their winds, we know that it's not our story.

I think for most of us because of that, we tend to lull ourselves to sleep at the wheel of life with thoughts like, "well, I'm not being abused or living all that uncomfortably, so I guess this boring marriage is where I stay." "What I have is fine or at least I have a job and I'm not homeless— look at how many people don't." "I should just shut up and take what they give me and be grateful", et cetera, et cetera. We tend to opt out of the magnificent for the mediocre because we have convinced ourselves that since we don't have the dramatic challenges, we should just be satisfied with what we have. It's not so bad, right?

But now it feels like telling my "non story" is a critical mission for me— where I'm basically demonstrating that those boring or unremarkable challenges still have the ability to erode our lives, still have the ability to cause us to play small, to discount our worth to put ourselves last, ultimately resulting in a life that always feels just a little bit off, always just a little unsatisfying, without the magic we crave.

My non story sends a message to all those women who just like me have justified staying on autopilot because we "weren't suffering enough" that our plight is, in fact, just as important and just as fixable with the potential for us to create lives that we're madly in love with and frankly, a sense of gratefulness that we're able to do this without having had to suffer through great tragedy or challenge to deserve it. Our middle of the road lives are just as worthy of finding full self expression.

And now I feel really inspired as I do this work, to record what I'm learning, record what I'm seeing, write about it, take photographs, share that with you. My own journey to brave is a way to show you that you also deserve to have your own journey to brave, that allows you to be bold and resilient and authentic and vulnerable and always, always evolving.

A BRAVE Breath

"Your longing is valid. Your story matters."

The First Whispers of Restlessness

"Awakening begins as an irritation you can't explain—
and can't ignore."

Before the unraveling, before the collapse, before the lifequakes...
there were whispers.

Whispers disguised as irritations.

As questions that lingered long after I tried to silence them.
As small moments of misalignment that didn't seem worth
examining— until they began stacking on top of each other.

Awakening rarely announces itself.
It taps.
It nudges.
It unsettles.

For years, I felt like I was living inside a life that technically worked
but didn't quite fit.
A life built from checkboxes and expectations.
A life that looked exactly how it "should" look— but didn't feel like
mine.

I wasn't miserable.
I wasn't broken.
I wasn't even unhappy.
I was just... not alive.

And because I didn't have a dramatic crisis to point to, I dismissed
those whispers.
I minimized them.
I rationalized them.
I told myself I was lucky, privileged, successful— who was I to want
more?

But the body always knows before the mind catches up. The soul
always whispers before it screams. My whisper didn't come from a

grand epiphany. It came from noticing the growing distance between the woman I was performing and the woman I wanted to be.

Awakening begins with that distance— and the courage to admit you can feel it.

A BRAVE Breath

"The whisper you've been ignoring is the truth you've been seeking."

Why It's Important to Tell My Story Now

"Because silence keeps women lonely— and stories set us free."

After many years of hiding what I saw as failures so that I could show up in the world as worthy to mentor and coach others – I have realized that pretending to be someone I am not – giving the appearance that I am never wrong, things always work out for me, I am powerful at all times, etc. sets a false bar for those who look to me for guidance and support. And frankly, it's exhausting to keep up the façade. My facades became quite sophisticated as I created force fields around myself to ensure I could not be seen for who I really was.

I gained a lot of weight – and I think that was a way for me to prove myself right that I was not worthy of being loved or noticed – and a way to ensure I was dismissed and not paid attention to very closely. If nobody was looking, they wouldn't see my failure or my weaknesses. It also served as a force field to protect me from rejection and harm.

I took on more and more "exotic and exciting" jobs that turned me into a road warrior with a bigger and bigger paycheck – always on the go, always off doing some big, glamorous thing – as a way to compensate for the deficit in my physical health, my problematic relationships and my complete denial of the work and life that would feed my soul if I had dared to be honest with myself. I became so good at deflecting through achievement that I even moved to another continent on my own without my husband as part of my career skyrocket.

As a planner and someone who thrives on order – everything clean and crisp and in its place – I have struggled with the messiness of life and growing and reinventing. I have struggled with feelings of failure and frustration when my meticulous 100 step plan didn't actually go as

I planned. I took an all or nothing mindset that said if even one step was wrong or out of place – if one thing fell in a heap on the floor outside of its designated box – then the whole thing was a loss. A failure.

Because of this, I have stayed in relationships far past when I should have (either so I wouldn't have another failure on my "scorecard" or because I thought if I sacrificed enough or put enough effort in, I could save it.) When in fact what really happened is I compromised my own identity and my own needs for the sake of the win – for the sake of the relationship. Not only did this cause me to be unhappy, disappointed, or even emotionally damaged because I was unable to be my authentic self – but in doing so I became someone other than who the other person in the relationship "signed on" with.

All of those things that attracted the person into my life fell away in my pursuit of just making it work. In other relationships, I sabotaged them when the pain of watching the other person actually fully expressing themselves authentically became too painful for me to witness because I wasn't doing that myself. At the time I saw these people as annoying, entitled, self-involved . . .I now realize it was a just harsh mirror reflecting back to me the things that I was ignoring and starving in my own heart.

Because of this, I have stayed in jobs and work environments where I had to edit myself, or keep quiet and not rock the boat, or act in ways that were counter to my nature, or even push down my own ethical boundaries – to the point that I felt depressed, empty inside, numb . . . but was so afraid to be not liked or to not succeed or to lose a paycheck (and never find another one) that I just powered through it and pretended everything was ok. When I think about the number of people who were watching me and thinking there must be something wrong with THEM because they could not navigate those waters in the "successful" way I was – I am horrified.

A BRAVE Breath

"Your story doesn't need perfection— it needs permission."

When the Universe Whispered Back

"Sometimes the whisper becomes a question—
the kind you can't unhear."

Awakening rarely comes from one moment. It comes from a build-up of truths gathering courage inside you. But if I had to choose a single moment that shifted my axis, it was a seemingly ordinary day.

I was advocating for others, standing up to behaviors that weren't right, using my voice publicly… yet still searching for my own internal anchor.

And then it happened— not a lightning bolt, but a quiet click inside my chest:

"I am the one living this life.
So why am I still waiting for someone else to authorize it?"

It wasn't defiant.
It wasn't angry.
It was simply true.

That question cracked open a new truth: I had spent decades trusting everything *but* myself.

I trusted rules.
I trusted expectations.
I trusted systems never built for my heart.
I trusted people who loved the version of me that kept them comfortable.

But I did not trust me.

When that "click" happened— that quiet question about trusting my own truth— it didn't feel liberating. It felt terrifying.

Choosing myself meant I might lose the people who preferred the accommodating, predictable, high-achieving version of me. It meant stepping away from the validation I had built my identity upon.

It meant grieving the woman I had been — even if she was built on survival.

I remember thinking:

"If I choose myself... what if no one chooses me back?"

I also remember feeling the anxiety rise in my chest as I confronted the abusive, demoralizing behavior that had pushed me to the breaking point in the first place. No one wants to be "that person" — the one who disrupts the well-oiled machine, the one who speaks up, the one who stops staying quiet to keep the peace.

But the alternative— abandoning myself again— felt like a slow death.

This is the secret no one tells you:

Choosing yourself doesn't feel brave at first.
It feels like loss.
It feels like fear.
It feels like the beginning of a life you don't yet know how to live.

But it is the most honest choice you will ever make.

And the truth, once heard, is impossible to unhear.

Awakening begins with that question:
What if I trusted myself first?

A BRAVE Breath

"The first act of courage is listening to the truth you've already spoken inside yourself."

WAYPOINT TWO — THE UNRAVELING

Where what falls apart reveals what was never true.

The Unraveling is the stage where everything you've been holding together starts to fall apart. This is the breakdown before the breakthrough. The structures you've built— the identities, the relationships, the beliefs, the routines— begin to crack and crumble. What was once solid feels unstable. What was once clear becomes confusing. You're not falling apart because you're weak. You're falling apart because what you built was never meant to last. It was built on someone else's foundation, and now your authentic self is demanding space.

When Strong Stops Working

"Strength becomes a cage when it requires your self-abandonment."

There comes a moment when the version of you who could push through anything simply can't anymore.

For me, it happened on a day that blurred into the next— a stretch of time where I stayed curled under a comforter, not showering, not moving, not entirely sure what day it was.

The most effort I could muster was sending my cousin a quick "proof of life" text, not because I wanted connection, but because I needed to convince her not to come over and witness the shape I was in.

I didn't know if I was sick or depressed or simply incapable of functioning anymore.

But I knew one thing with frightening clarity: the woman who had held everything together for decades had finally hit a wall her willpower could not climb.

I felt embarrassed by my exhaustion. Angry that I wasn't "stronger." Ashamed that I couldn't keep performing the version of myself everyone depended on.

It felt as if the world had watched me fail and quietly stepped back. My worst fear rose in my chest: I don't belong. I'm not worthy. I am not enough.

But here's the truth I couldn't see then: strength was never the problem. The problem was the cost.

I had built a life that rewarded me for resilience, endurance, and carrying more than my share . . . but it demanded a silence that was killing me.

That day under the comforter wasn't a collapse. It was an awakening disguised as surrender.

It was the moment I began to understand that strength is not sustainable when it requires the abandonment of self.

A BRAVE Breath

"You're allowed to stop carrying what was never yours to hold."

About Being Brave

"Bravery isn't the absence of fear— it's choosing truth anyway."

There's a particular kind of bravery that doesn't look brave at all.

It looks like showing up on the day you want to disappear.

It looks like telling the truth when you'd rather stay quiet.

It looks like letting yourself be seen in the middle of the mess, not after you've cleaned it up.

Most of us were taught that bravery means powering through. Pushing down the tears. Staying productive. Being "fine."

But real bravery— the kind that changes your life— often begins the moment you admit you're not fine.

It's the moment you stop fighting your own humanity.

It's the moment you let your pain be real.

It's the moment you say: "I can't do this the way I've been doing it."

And instead of judging yourself for it… you listen.

That's what unraveling does.

It strips the performance away until all that's left is truth.

And that's where bravery lives— not in perfection, but in honesty.

For a number of years now, I have been told by friends or people who observe me living my life that I am "brave"— that I have courage to do a number of the things that I've done, particularly over the last three or four years or so. And for a while, I really cringed at being seen in that way. I really cringed at being called brave. I wanted to dismiss it. I wanted to call it something else. I wanted to make it smaller or less significant.

I have found that as I reflected on the times when people said that about me, that a lot of where that reaction came from was in my mind. I never felt brave. I never felt courageous. Oftentimes when I've made big moves in my life where I get that response, I'm actually absolutely terrified inside. I am afraid, I'm unsure. And in some ways, I felt a level of shame or embarrassment, or that I was some sort of impostor. I was faking it for all of these people that observed me being brave. I've tried to work through this in my mind over the last few years about how to reconcile and honor other people's opinions and their observations about the world and about me.

Many of you know that brave for me has become a bit of an acronym for how I believe we should be showing up in the world. To me, brave stands for bold, resilient, authentic, vulnerable and evolving. If we can really aspire to do those five things, it will lead us to do things that do appear brave, that do appear courageous. Also, it's ok to be completely terrified inside because what you're really doing is you're stepping into that place of discomfort. The "dis" in discomfort stands for "do it still." That's where true bravery and courage come from. It's not that you're not afraid. It's not that you have no fear. It's that you do it still. You step into discomfort, and you do that until it becomes comfortable— discomfort becomes comfort, unfamiliar becomes familiar. That's how you do that. It's a muscle that you exercise.

This can be really hard for us. I don't think it's necessarily that we can't get past that fear to do the brave or courageous act. I don't think it's always because we doubt that we have the skills to do it. I think on some level, we know that as humans, we are resilient enough to recover from a lot of mistakes. But I think we do tend to have a level of shame and an aversion to vulnerability that says if I am seen, if I do this thing and I am seen and I fail, I will be embarrassed. And that's almost a worse life sentence than the failure itself. It's the being embarrassed that other people saw the failure.

47

Other people might shake their heads, click their tongue, or say look at that person, they look ridiculous. I think it is that self-preservation that our ego has that is really the source of that fear.

Because when we can quiet down the ego that is genuinely trying to protect us, genuinely trying to preserve our sense of self by not letting us get in tricky situations or by not allowing us to look stupid or allowing us to look incompetent or all of these other things that it tells us that it's doing in that loud voice it has that serves to drown out the small voice inside of you that absolutely knows without a doubt that you are smart enough, that you are capable enough, that you can overcome any challenge put in front of you.

But that voice is really, really hard to hear. When you think about making changes in your life, you must wake up that limb that's asleep, and you've got those pins and needles as you come out of autopilot. You attempt to make some little changes— but even little changes can feel really big to you if it's the first time you've come out of autopilot in a while. The reaction you get inside may feel quite negative compared to the external validation that you are getting. But if you do start to get those positive external reactions that say, wow, you know, you're so brave, you're so courageous— you may start to feel that sense of embarrassment or shame that someone's thinking that you are brave and courageous when you still don't feel that way inside. I want you to remember what I've said. You have the fear, but you're stepping into the discomfort and you're going to do it still.

That really is part of the journey to brave— understanding this and keeping in the acronym in mind as you go. Be bold. You don't need to ask anybody's permission. You have complete agency over yourself and how you think, do and show up in the world. Be resilient. You are going to have to be because nobody is perfect. The world is not perfect, and stuff happens that we don't have control over and we just have to bounce back. Be authentic. Be your truest self. Being authentic is where you're going to find your people, it's when you're going to find your path and all of the other stuff that has surrounded you while you are on autopilot— not being your authentic self— is going to fall away. Be vulnerable. You have to let people in. You have to let the universe in. We have to stop hiding from each other because it turns out we're all hiding the same things.

We are all more similar than we are different, but we're so conditioned now through social media and other avenues that we have to create and polish things in such a way that so that they're acceptable, that we forget that if we're vulnerable, we're going to find other people who have the same crazy thoughts, who have the same challenges, who want the same achievement and success and joy and contentment in their lives. And those are the people who can support us. It's a game changer and you're never going to get there without being vulnerable. And finally, continue to evolve. You cannot stay stagnant. If you stop moving and growing, you're dying. You have to evolve.

You get new information every second of every day and it changes you in some way and you are a different person Every bit of input, physical, emotional, intellectual and mental that comes into you makes you different. It evolves you and you have to be open to that. You have to seek that out. You have to crave that because that is the only way that you move forward and get out of autopilot. On your journey to brave, just remember that and just take those little steps that get you there through the discomfort. Do it still!

A BRAVE Breath

"You don't have to be strong all the time. You just have to be honest."

Transforming Through Life's Curveballs

"The world doesn't always give you clean endings. Sometimes it gives you curveballs— and asks who you want to become next."

There are some obvious patterns in how I've moved through the biggest curveballs of my life— especially my divorces. Both of my marriages lasted over a decade. Both endings disrupted everything: my relationships, my living situation, and my career. And both divorces were initiated under eerily similar circumstances— betrayal, shock, and the sudden collapse of a life I thought I understood.

In my first marriage, we had just returned from Key West where we renewed our vows for our ten-year anniversary. We were there with our five-year-old son, surrounded by friends and the quirky performing community we were part of— pirate entertainers, musicians, artists.

My husband stayed an extra week in Florida to pursue a work opportunity for our company. When he finally came home, everything seemed normal. We picked him up from the airport, went to brunch, laughed, came home, and took naps like any other ordinary family day.

I woke up first. And for reasons I still can't fully explain, I walked into the kitchen, went to our family computer, and started digging through archived chat logs.

Almost in slow motion, I found them.

A long conversation between my husband and a woman we knew through our performing circle- someone who had been in our home before. Their messages were unmistakable.

They were having an affair. And they were planning what came next. I felt like the world dropped out from under me. I spent hours trying to get him to confess on his own, hoping he would do the honorable thing without me forcing it. But he didn't. Eventually, I confronted him.

Over the following weeks we fought, cried, went silent, and tried to make sense of what was happening. I asked him to stop seeing her and go to counseling. He refused.

A few weeks later, he packed one of our cars and moved to Florida to be with her— leaving just before our son's sixth birthday. And because we ran a company together, I didn't just lose my marriage. I lost my career, too.

In the wreckage of that first divorce, I did what a lot of women do: I started rebuilding before I had even fully processed the loss. I stayed in the family home and kept my married name for a year so my son wouldn't feel his entire world change overnight. Then I sold the house and moved us into a rental on the water . . .a place with views of ferries and the Seattle skyline. It became a kind of sanctuary.

I cobbled together work— first with friends, then with connections— but some of those paths ended painfully. Ethical concerns, broken trust, friendships dissolving. Even the performing group I once loved fell apart.

Eventually, I found stable work at Boeing. I started as a contractor, figured out how to work the system, and was hired as a full employee within five months. I bought my first home as a single mom, and I was incredibly proud of that. Then I went back to school for my MBA. As a single mom. While working full-time. And during all of it, I lost almost ninety pounds. So much weight that I eventually had surgery to remove excess skin.

Looking back now, I see what I was really doing. Yes, I was building a life. But I was also trying to prove something.

That I could survive.
That I could recover.
That I was still worthy.

I met my second husband through a close friend— someone who helped me through the first divorce, someone I loved deeply, even if I often felt like I had to compromise myself to stay connected.

When my second marriage ended, it didn't come out of nowhere. There had been questionable contact with other women for years — not always overt, but enough to make my stomach drop more than once. I confronted him when it happened, but I also dismissed my instincts and accepted apologies. Because somewhere inside me, I didn't want another failed marriage on my scorecard.

And then – after I returned from Australia, already emotionally fragile— my husband dropped a truth I wasn't prepared for. He told me he needed, at minimum, an open marriage to be happy. Ideally, he wanted polyamory— another man or woman inside our intimate circle.

I was heartbroken.

I went away for a long weekend to think. And in that desperate place— desperate not to fail again— came home and agreed to try it, with strict boundaries. I wasn't excited. I wasn't comfortable. But I convinced myself I was being open-minded and loving.

Two days later, we were in the dog park, and he handed me his phone to show me something. A text popped up from a woman's name I didn't recognize. And again, almost like slow motion, I clicked it. I scrolled. And what I found was unmistakable: he didn't just know her. He knew her well. Intimately. And he had been building that connection long before he ever mentioned open marriage to me.

He lied at first — said he had just met her, that he was "starting the process." Then slowly he admitted the truth: he'd been cultivating it for months.

Something inside me snapped.

It wasn't just the betrayal. It was the realization that I had been bending myself to save a marriage that he had been quietly dismantling behind my back. And then he said terrible things about me — the kind of things you should never hear from the person who is supposed to love you most.

That was my breaking point. Because I could survive betrayal. But I could not survive being degraded and destroyed by the person who claimed to be my partner.

Later, I learned he had been sleeping with that woman while we were still living together . . . while I was trying to rebuild myself after Australia.

And all those moments I ignored my gut? Turns out I was right.

This happened days before the first COVID lockdown in March 2020. We tried to live "separated" in a one-bedroom apartment during full lockdown. It was unbearable. After six weeks, on Easter Sunday, I packed my car with what I could fit and drove to my cousin's cottage on Cape Cod.

Not long after, I learned I was likely facing a layoff. Rather than wait for the company to decide my future, I took the voluntary option and reclaimed my power. I didn't just need a new marriage. I needed a new life. I went back to school. Got certified to teach English internationally. Got my Massachusetts real estate license.

My plan was to move overseas— but COVID shut that down. So instead, I started applying for jobs again. Eventually, it came down to three options: a rocket company in Denver, a tech company in DC, or a position back at my former company that would relocate me to Southern California. I chose California.

Not because it was perfect, but because I needed a clean slate. I needed distance from my old life, and I wanted to live by the ocean. So in September 2020, I moved to the beach In January 2021, I started coach training. And within eighteen months of leaving that DC apartment, I had:

— rebuilt my life again
— hanged careers
— moved across the country
— lost sixty pounds
— built new community
— and stepped into a version of myself I didn't even know was possible.

For a long time, I resisted sharing my story. Because I didn't think it was dramatic enough. I had seen the "hero's journey" stories— the ones that feel like movies. The ones with dramatic trauma and sparkly turning points. My life didn't look like that. I hadn't been homeless, brutalized, or overtly discriminated against. I hadn't battled catastrophic illness. I didn't have one single defining moment that explained everything.

So I thought: who am I to tell my story? But then a quiet voice came through: The unremarkable story is the story.

Most women don't have Lifetime-Movie lives. We have "fine" lives. We have "not so bad" lives. We have lives that quietly erode us — and we don't notice until something falls apart. And that's why it matters. Because the women who are staying in mediocre marriages, soul-sucking jobs, or half-lived versions of themselves— not because it's unbearable, but because it's tolerable — and they just need someone to say:

You are not broken.
You are not dramatic.
You are waking up.

This is why I do what I do now. Not because I'm extraordinary. But because I've lived the way so many women live: shutting down, performing strength, ignoring truth, and convincing myself I should be grateful for less.

BRAVE isn't a personality trait. It's a practice. Bold. Resilient. Authentic. Vulnerable. Evolving. And I've lived enough curveballs to know this:

Sometimes life doesn't give you a clean path forward. Sometimes it gives you a collapse— and asks you to rise anyway.

A BRAVE Breath

"Your life doesn't have to be dramatic to be worthy of transformation."

Adventures and Gaslighting at the Bottom of the World

"Sometimes the most magical chapter of your life contains the deepest scar."

My year in Australia was one of the most exciting, fulfilling, transformative— and tragic— times of my life.

For years I had wanted an overseas assignment through my company, but those opportunities were rare and competitive. I assumed it might never happen. Then the planets aligned.

The right role appeared, it fit my skill set perfectly, and it was in Australia! I leveraged every connection I had just to get an interview— and then I did what I always do when I want something badly.

I prepared like my life depended on it. I researched the market, the business landscape, the culture, the internal stakeholders. I walked into that interview with energy that practically radiated out of my laptop screen. I had to consciously rein myself in so I didn't come across as *too* excited.

Waiting for the decision was torture. I was on vacation with my husband over the Fourth of July when I got the call: The job was mine. We were moving to Australia. I was beyond excited.

A few months later, the first shoe dropped. My husband was offered his own dream job, one that required deployment to places like Afghanistan and Africa for months at a time. After long conversations, we decided to pursue both opportunities. We put him on my visa, knowing the reality: I would spend the first year in Australia alone The plan was that he would join me in year two.

I moved Thanksgiving weekend 2018. He stayed behind. And in March 2019, he deployed to Afghanistan for six months. And just like that, I was alone in Brisbane . . . on the adventure I had dreamed about for years.

Brisbane was everything I hoped for: beautiful, sunny, wrapped around a river that cut through the heart of the city. I found an apartment in a park-like neighborhood built during a World's Fair— walkable cafes, restaurants, and shops, with a rooftop pool that had panoramic views of the skyline. My daily commute became a 30-minute walk across a pedestrian bridge, through botanical gardens, and into the central business district. It felt like I had stepped into an alternate version of my own life. One where the world was wide, and I was brave enough to live inside it.

The single best thing I did in Australia wasn't professional. It was personal. I joined the book club in my apartment building. That might sound small, but for me it was huge. I had never been naturally skilled at making new female friendships as an adult. But I knew I was in a new country where I knew *no one*— and if I didn't put myself out there, I would disappear into isolation.

The first night I showed up, only one woman came: Julie, the organizer. I was nervous. The kind of nervous where your brain scrambles for small talk and your body looks for an escape route. But something beautiful happened. We clicked. That book club became my lifeline— a core group of six women who anchored me through everything. Half Australian, some British and Irish, and me: the only American. We grew from book discussions into real friendship— happy hours, hikes, concerts, weekends away, brunches, and deep conversations that left me feeling seen in ways I hadn't experienced in years. I still consider them one of the greatest gifts of my life.

And they taught me something I hadn't fully realized before: Vulnerability is the gateway to belonging.

At first, my job felt like a dream. The role had room for me to make my mark. My American network and experience were valued. The team was strong, welcoming, and socially connected. I made fast friends. I was still pinching myself.

But there was a shadow in the room from the beginning. My boss. He was charismatic, good-looking, charming, magnetic— the kind of leader who knows exactly how to win people over. He also carried an inflated ego, the kind that doesn't fully reveal itself until the shine wears off. It only took a couple months before I began seeing what was underneath.

He ignored basic company rules. He used the geographic distance from the U.S. to operate however he pleased. He had contempt for "the Americans," yet depended on them to advance his own status. At first I raised questions privately— genuinely trying to understand whether certain procedures translated differently in Australia. But it became clear: he knew exactly what he was doing. And he didn't appreciate being questioned.

The work environment became a psychological minefield. He controlled everything: who we spoke to, what we said, what meetings we could request. We had to get permission to schedule appointments, get slide decks approved, and eventually even submit word-for-word scripts of what we planned to say.

The message underneath it all was clear: You are not trusted. You are not capable. You are not safe.

He used humiliation and intimidation as management tactics. People were coached before meetings on what questions to ask to win his favor and what not to say so they wouldn't be publicly destroyed. He would walk into all-hands meetings late, like a performer waiting for his audience to fill the room. And you could feel it: the air sucked out of the space the moment he arrived.

People were afraid. I became the informal therapist for the team. People cried in my office. People doubted their competence, questioned their intelligence, and wondered if they were losing their minds. And that's when I realized what was happening. This wasn't leadership. This was abuse.

Gaslighting is insidious. It doesn't start with cruelty— it starts with confusion. It starts with small corrections that make you question your memory, your judgment, your worth. It's like the frog in boiling water: you don't notice the temperature rising until you're already sinking. I saw him give clear instructions to employees, only to berate them the following week for doing exactly what he asked. The room would go silent. Everyone saw what happened. No one spoke up. The fear was that deep. I began to wonder daily: Am I actually stupid? Am I crazy?

That's what gaslighting does. It makes you doubt yourself until you become compliant.

And I also came to understand something else:

He hated that I was better connected to the American side of the company than he was. He began trashing my reputation behind my back. Whisper campaigns. Doubt. Isolation. He tried to poison my relationships with key stakeholders and even my peers. Some connections survived. Others were obliterated. And something in me began to break.

By July 2019, I was done. I didn't care about status. I didn't care about career trajectory. I was at the point where I would rather quit and sleep on the streets of Brisbane than endure one more day. So I went to HR.

I learned they were at least partly aware of his behavior, and that other investigations might already be underway. They connected me with the President of the Australia business— someone who had been in conflict with my boss and wanted to support me. We scheduled a meeting. It was supposed to happen the day before a long holiday weekend.

At the last minute, we rescheduled it for after the break. And then he died in a boating accident. Just like that, my most powerful ally against my boss was gone. To this day, I still cannot wrap my mind around the brutality of that timing.

I began reaching out to every contact I had in the U.S., searching for a landing spot. Most people didn't seem to grasp how bad it was. And I was watching the truth happen in real time: If you don't have power or connections, the system can swallow you whole.

Eventually my former boss— a high-ranking executive— stepped in and brought me home. He essentially hid me in a temporary position to buy me time, but it came at a huge cost:

  I lost my second year in Australia
  I accepted a two-level demotion
  I returned home damaged, shaken, and scarred

I moved back in November 2019— four months after I begged for help.

The months that followed were the hardest to explain. On the outside, I had "escaped." But inside, I was shattered. I agreed to file a formal ethics complaint – ten pages, nearly thirty recommended witnesses— and still, in the end, nothing happened. The case was deemed not "solid enough." And my boss? He got promoted. That was its own kind of trauma: the realization that truth doesn't always win.

I finally started therapy in January 2020. Two months later: the pandemic. Then my job became unstable. Then my marriage imploded. Australia wasn't just the beginning of the end of my corporate career. It was the beginning of the end of my marriage, too.

But here is the strange truth: Despite everything, Australia is still the favorite place I've ever lived. It was magical.

I made the most of my time there. I explored Brisbane relentlessly. I became an Aussie Rules Football fan and went to nearly every Brisbane Lions game. I traveled whenever I could— the Gold Coast, Sydney, Melbourne, Cairns, the Great Barrier Reef, the rainforest, Uluru, the middle of the country. And I did it all without a car. My Australian friends would laugh and tell me I'd seen more of their country than they had— and they were born there. Australia expanded me. Even as it scarred me. Both can be true.

Australia taught me that:

- **belonging requires vulnerability** (that book club changed my life)

- **adventure builds self-trust** (especially when you do it alone)

- **being a guest in another culture humbles you** (and expands empathy fast)

- **asking for help is strength** (not weakness)

- and that no job, no leader, no system is worth sacrificing your mental health

And if there is a "Boss" in your life— someone who manipulates, gaslights, devalues, isolates, or sabotages you- hear me clearly:

Do not doubt yourself.

You are always right about how you feel. Even if it turns out to be a misunderstanding, your feelings are real. And they deserve attention. Speak up. Find an ally— or a gang of allies. Ask for help sooner than you want to. And if you need to, remove yourself immediately. Because you can never go wrong when you choose to show up for yourself.

Ever.

A BRAVE Breath

"The moment you stop doubting yourself is the moment you become unbreakable."

The Cost of Holding It All Together

"Unraveling isn't the breaking— it's the truth escaping its container."

There's a particular heartbreak that comes when the life you built collapses from two directions at once.

My marriage fractured in one hand, my career dissolved in the other— but instead of anger, the first thing I felt was shame.

Shame that I didn't see it sooner. Shame that I couldn't hold it together. Shame that I must have done something wrong.

I was the common denominator, so who else could I blame but myself?

Betrayal has a way of making you question your worth, your instincts, your very identity.

I wasn't just losing a husband or a job title— I was losing the version of myself who believed she could outwork, outperform, or "be good enough" to keep her world intact.

The collapse of my marriage and career didn't just break my life open . . . it dismantled my identity.

But here is the truth I couldn't have known yet: sometimes your life has to fall apart so you can stop holding up the pieces that were never meant to be yours.

Unraveling isn't failure. It's release.

It's the moment the pressure of holding everything together becomes heavier than the fear of letting go.

A BRAVE Breath

"Sometimes the life you lose is the one that was breaking you."

The Mirror and the Reckoning

"Self-abandonment is the quietest heartbreak— and the first one we learn to ignore."

The hardest part of unraveling wasn't the loss.
It wasn't the betrayal.
It wasn't even the grief.

It was the mirror

The truth no one told me?
It is harder to look at yourself in the mirror— really look— than anyone expects.

Not the quick glance you give while rushing out the door.
Not the polite smile you practice convincing yourself you're okay.

The real look.
The one that lingers.
The one that refuses to turn away.

It was realizing that the woman staring back at me— exhausted, grieving, stripped of all her defenses— was someone I had abandoned long before anyone else did.

The first time I really looked at myself, I didn't recognize the woman staring back.

Her eyes carried fatigue I had ignored.
Her face held grief she had never admitted.
Her body reflected years spent performing strength instead of feeling anything real.

She was familiar, yet distant.
Hopeful, yet frightened.
Visible, yet hidden beneath decades of expectations.

She wasn't broken.
She was buried.

And beneath the exhaustion, I saw something else— something I wasn't prepared for:

A flicker of hope.
A quiet question.
A possibility.

The mirror showed me the truth I'd been avoiding— that I had been living as a version of myself created for survival, not for joy.
For acceptance, not for authenticity.
For belonging, but not for wholeness.

I cried for her . . .not out of despair, but recognition.
Because for the first time, she felt seen.

In that moment, the woman in the mirror whispered back to me:

"I am the one you've been waiting for.
I've been waiting for you to choose me."

Reckoning is not self-blame.
Reckoning is self-recognition.

It's the moment you stop looking outward for the cause of your pain and begin looking inward for the truth of your becoming.

Unraveling isn't the end.
It's the first honest moment.

Awakening is not about fixing yourself.
It's the moment you finally acknowledge your own reflection and say, "I'm willing to begin."

A BRAVE Breath

"The moment you see yourself clearly is the moment you return to yourself."

WAYPOINT THREE — THE RECKONING

Where you stop performing— and start choosing yourself.

The Reckoning is the stage where you stop running from the truth and finally turn to face it. This is where you look at your life— your choices, your relationships, your patterns, your complicity— and you name what is. Not what you wish it were. Not what it looks like from the outside. What it actually is. The Reckoning is honest, and honesty is rarely comfortable. But this is where your power returns. Because you can't change what you won't acknowledge.

What is an Identity Anyway?

"Your identity is what you were taught to be— until you choose who you truly are."

What is an identity? What does that even mean when we are talking about it? And even if I know what an identity is— or what my identity is— is that something I need to reclaim? Am I missing out on something here?

I think we have all had these questions. It is legit. So let's start with a basic, shared understanding.

When I say *identity*, I mean the memories and experiences, relationships, beliefs, and values that create our sense of self. It includes all the definitions and rules— and even the perceived boundaries or limitations— that shape who we are. It is also entirely individual: what makes up my identity will not be the same as what makes up yours. And it directs not only how we see ourselves, but how we see our communities, the world, and how we fit into it.

Often, identity is shaped by both internal and external factors. Over time, it becomes an internal monologue that shows up externally in how we behave, function, and move through life. At its core, identity is built on our belief system . . . the things that tell us what is right and wrong, what is true and false, what is acceptable or even virtuous, or not. Our beliefs give us direction. They are our way of learning how to navigate the world... or not.

I say that our belief system is comprised of both internal and external components. When I speak about external factors, I'm talking about things outside of ourselves that we use as measures of acceptability or models of sameness or comparison to help us understand "where we fit in." These are often related to things like the job we have or the place we live, our role or status in our circle of friends or the car we drive, the followers on our Instagram feed, where we went to school, and the places we volunteer. You get the idea. Now, at some point in this conversation, we are going to dive into how much weight those external things really should have in your identity. But for now, we are just going to set those aside, because what I really want to focus on right now are those internal factors that make up your identity.

The internal factors are initially those beliefs around our big rocks like spirituality or connection to that which is greater, affinity for country of origin or race, perhaps rules and definitions for being a good or virtuous person, attitudes or norms about money or family structure or age or gender. Maybe I say initially because we don't create our own beliefs at the beginning, we inherit them. Spoiler alert, this is why ultimately, we have the power (and I will go so far as to say the responsibility) to be eyes wide open as grownups to assess, reassess, and curate the beliefs that we allow to stand as the ingredients for our identities. We'll get to that. So that's a lot to take in at a first swipe of how we get to an identity and why it might be possibly something we want to reclaim, which we haven't quite delved into yet. So how does this even happen? How does this even start, this identity that we might want to reclaim?

The ingredients of our identity are this belief system that we inherit as children. It's what I'll call a starter pack of beliefs from our family of origin, whatever that looks like. Let's illustrate that in one of the more common scenarios. You are a child in a family with parents or caretakers. I'll use those terms interchangeably. Those caretakers in the course of raising you as a child give you a set of beliefs, their beliefs, because that's what they know. They also got their beliefs from their families of origin and so on through generations and hundreds and probably thousands of years.

Each generation adds their own layers of experience and interpretation to this pack of beliefs. And that's just the way of the world. So you're given this set of beliefs, and your parents are your whole world. So, of course, you take those beliefs as gospel. That's just the way the world is and that confidence in those beliefs is what as a child keeps you feeling safe and knowing that you belong and that you're doing the right thing within your family unit, within your community. This is how it goes for all of us. It's how we all begin.

Then as you begin to mature as a child, eventually, you get to a point where you begin to be able to critically think. You begin to be able to look at concepts and ideas and break them down and really start to think through them and do more of this thinking for yourself, more questioning. Now, you're probably thinking to yourself — Ok. Well, that means that at that point, I am ready to change my mind about everything. Maybe I could do whatever I want. Well, you probably can, but it's likely that you don't. I mean, you probably question and rebel and act out. It's what children do as they explore their boundaries. But since your beliefs have shaped your identity, you do not actually end up straying too far from them. Or if you do, it is rarely sustainable long term, because the internal drive to be aligned and the external pressure to assimilate are strong. And here's why. (Well, one of the reasons why.)

The view of the world that your belief system colors in for you really informs you who you need to be in that world. All of those beliefs have now shaped this person who you now must live up to, or down to, depending on what reality your belief system has designed. Let's not forget that all of our identities that we've experienced so far in our lives have not necessarily been superstar . . . Sometimes the identities that have been formed are very negative in nature, but we will try to prove those right too. It really depends on where we come from. But it's not something we can ignore either as a human. We all need to have an identity.

For most of us, that means going along with what we think is our one and only option, the one we were given or born with, so to speak. And what we find when we live in a life like that is that often, we have to compromise on those little niggling voices that are telling us, maybe

70

we think differently, maybe we are different, maybe we want something different, but we have to push those down, right? Because that can't possibly be correct. My belief system says something else.

So, we go about working through the tick list of things that our belief system tells us are the indicators of being a successful and therefore worthy human— the job, the possessions, the lifestyle, the achievements, the family structure that we are supposed to have and should feel very accomplished and proud of ourselves about getting. And if those things are not, in fact, in alignment with the identity inside us that wants to come through— which frankly, we probably do not even know is happening to us in the moment— then we beat ourselves up because we do not feel the way that we are supposed to feel. We are bored with it. We are uncomfortable with it. We are unsatisfied with it.

And immediately our reflection comes back to us and says: there must be something wrong with us. Because our belief system says this is what we should be striving for. This is what we should be proud of. This is what brings us joy and safety. This is what will bring us love.

Your ego is always there in the background. It was just waiting for its chance to shine. Your ego who has this job to keep you safe, to keep you "right." As you get older and you get into this mode where you can critically think, you look at those beliefs and your ego wants you to be right. So your ego, because we do not know that we need to be on anything other than autopilot and just go along with our beliefs and whatever our internal monologue says, your ego is gathering evidence that your beliefs are true and correct.

You begin to develop this cognitive bias that you may not even realize that you have. And so it goes as you are progressing through your childhood into early adulthood. Basically your ego's mission is to find all the evidence it can that your belief system is correct, that your belief system is right and solid. It's the way it is and that's what we do.

So whether it is the information that we take in from the world and filter through to the parts that make us right, or whether it is experiences that we have or actions that we take that seem to kind of set us up either to prove that our belief is true in a positive way— or when we try to do something outside of that belief and it goes terribly wrong to also prove to us the same thing with an "I told you so"— we are on a hell-bent mission to be right.

This is pretty much the human condition. And for many, many, many people— I would say most people— this is how we stumble or navigate our way through life. We are given a belief system, and we spend the rest of our lives on autopilot proving ourselves right. The good, the bad, and the ugly of it. And period, that's the end of the story.

I'll say it again for emphasis: we all need an identity. It makes me think of Game of Thrones. There was one episode where it was terrifyingly illustrated. There was this kind of monastery where the people had no faces. They were all generic. The whole point was that they had no identity in real life. That can be a scary place to be in.

I feel like I've tipped my toe into that at one point in my journey, when a large part of my identity was comprised of external factors. And when many of those fell away in a perfect storm of what I call lifequakes, I was lost and I felt like I had no identity. And for me, it was a terrible and scary place to be. It just seemed improbable— impossible, really— that I did not have an identity. It was a very low time in my life.

But the point is this: as humans, we all need an identity because it is that identity that allows us to figure out who our tribe is . . . where we fit in. In the beginning, it's with our families of origin. Then it is with our community, our society, our world. We need to know what our identity is because that is how we make a value judgment on where we belong and what we should be doing with this life that we have. So think about that in your own life. It's true, right?

72

There are aspects of all of this that work amazingly well for us. And there are aspects that do not. The aspects that work very well just reinforce our beliefs, and maybe rightly so. We have confirmed that our identity is good, our beliefs are good, everything is great.

Then come the challenges and struggles... or boredom... or failures. We explain those away in a number of different ways, still within the construct of the identity that we have and the belief system that we hold and believe to be true because our ego tells us it must be true. If you reflect on how you have moved through your life, you will inevitably find this to be true.

It is problematic to go through life on this sort of autopilot— which frankly, most of us do because it is what we know. It is what we have been taught. Nobody sets us up in a master class on how to think outside of our acceptable belief system. Nobody does that. Not when we are children. Not when we are teenagers. Not when we are in college, typically. But we are starting to see more opportunities for that kind of mind expansion.

These beliefs feel unmovable and unchangeable, largely because as humans, we need to feel safe and we need to belong. So, when we have those thoughts — "Isn't there more?" or "I guess this is all there is..."— we tend to override them. We assume this is the way it is. We must have that strife. We have to make that sacrifice. We must take that responsibility and do the right thing . . .all based through the lens of our belief system and our identity. It is the hamster wheel we all live on... until we do not.

To add yet another level of complexity, we are existing and growing in a world that continually gives us more input about what we should be doing, thinking, and feeling. Those ideas layer onto us— layer after layer— as the new thing or latest thing that it is going to take for us to be acceptable, to be successful, to belong. And when we are on autopilot, we just keep accepting them.

Then you arrive at midlife. And at this point, you have likely had an innumerable number of layers in your belief system that have insulated you from yourself in an effort to belong. Then something happens. Something shifts. Something falls apart. You lose a job, lose a loved one, become an empty nester, get a big promotion, get a divorce— whatever it is. Suddenly there is something inside you that says: "I do not feel comfortable in my own skin. What am I missing? Is this all there is? Who am I?"

You can call it a midlife crisis. I do not think it is a crisis. I think it is a call to action.

That is the moment where there is an invitation to reclaim your actual identity. The one that has nothing to do with the belief system you inherited and kept collecting artifacts of while you were on autopilot.

And here is the catch: you cannot reclaim that identity without looking at the belief system that created the one you are currently living in. It is all connected.

When you know something is out of alignment, the first thing we want to do is hit the easy button. Read the book. Take the course. Go on the retreat. Watch the YouTube video. Change the behavior. Change the habit. Do something different.

But you cannot have lasting behavior change without having the identity that supports it— which means looking at the belief system that created the identity.

Your beliefs are the ingredients for your identity. Your behaviors and habits are the external expression of that identity. You cannot sustain a behavior that conflicts with who you believe you are.

Let me be clear: that is not a commentary on your motivation or work ethic. That is simply the truth of how identity works.

This is really what I mean when I talk about reclaiming your identity. I am not talking about reclaiming the identity of your childhood, because even that was created with inherited beliefs.

But we are far enough along now. We have lived. We have experienced. We have seen enough to be in a well-informed position to go back and reevaluate all those layers of beliefs we have collected over time… and curate them.

The identity we are reclaiming is the one in that quiet voice, not the ego that yammers at us all day long.

And yes, letting go of old beliefs is scary. Because so many of our beliefs are tied to being acceptable. Being safe. Being in the club. Belonging.

But the work is deciding, as grown ass adults, which beliefs we keep, and which ones we lovingly release. "Thank you. You served your purpose. And now I let you go."

As we do that, and as we mindfully listen to that inner voice, the identity we really want begins to emerge. The beliefs that support it begin to coalesce. And where there are gaps, we go seek the knowledge we need to build a new, informed belief system— one that supports our authentic identity.

That is the identity you reclaim. Or maybe discover it for the first time.

And when you reclaim it, that is when your behaviors and habits finally have something solid to root into. That is when you begin to build a life that actually feels like yours.

A BRAVE Breath

"You are allowed to outgrow the version of you that was built to survive. Your identity is not a life sentence — it is a living, evolving truth."

Conforming for Comfort

"Belonging shouldn't cost you your truth."

The hardest part wasn't looking in the mirror— it was recognizing the woman staring back. I had abandoned myself long before anyone else ever did. And I could almost hear her whisper:

"I am the one you've been waiting for.
I've been waiting for you to choose me."

So let's talk about one of the most common ways we abandon ourselves — often without even realizing it. When we talk about belief systems, one of the things I see in play is this idea of *conforming for comfort.*

Ever heard of "The Conformity Bind"? Michelle King— author of *The Fix: Overcome the Invisible Barriers That Are Holding Women Back at Work*— uncovered this in her PhD research when she studied how companies define the "ideal employee" and how people achieve success within that definition. What she found was simple and kind of brutal: new employees often find the quickest path to success by conforming to the culture— and in many workplaces, those norms tend to be masculine in nature.

So what does that mean for women? It means we learn to dress, speak, and behave in ways that may be out of character — because it gives us access to social capital: mentors, sponsors, connections, opportunity, credibility. We build these facades because, in some environments, it feels like survival. But here's the part that matters most:

Denying your identity doesn't make it disappear.

Even when we work overtime to blend in, we still "stick out" in many instances simply because we're not the norm. And that creates what's often called hypervisibility— where your presence is more noticeable, and your behavior is more scrutinized. And for women of color, this can be amplified even further, because the "marks of otherness" stack. Now, what struck me is that what's true in corporate environments is also true in real life.

Think about it. Join a new church. Start a new job. Enter a new friend group. Go back to school. Walk into a new community space. There's always an "ideal." An unspoken template. A vibe. A code. A persona that seems to signal *this is how you belong here.*

And most of us— without even thinking about it— start adjusting ourselves to match it. We inherit belief systems. We learn what makes us accepted and safe. We scan the room, figure out the norms, and we model them. We do it to belong. At first, you usually don't want to stand out. It's not personal— it's primal. So yes, we conform for comfort. But here's what the research made crystal clear: conforming doesn't erase who you are— it just layers a mask over her. And at some point, those layers start to press down.

You feel uncomfortable in your own skin. You can't explain why, but something feels off. It's like you're living a life that technically works... but doesn't fit. There's a line from this research that hooked me:

"Trying to pretend to be someone else is an exhausting and demoralizing process."

Yes. That. Exactly. Because all of us— at one time or another (and for some of us, pretty much 24/7) have been conditioned into being someone we're not. And the longer we carry those facades, the heavier they get. Also... can we just pause for a second and acknowledge how close the words **conform** and **comfort** are? It's almost too on the nose.

I think conformity comes in two flavors: surface conformity and deep conformity Surface conformity is the stuff we do just to function in society. In the U.S., we drive on the right side of the road. We stand in line and wait our turn. We follow rules that keep things safe and orderly. That kind of conformity makes sense. But then there's another category of surface conformity that isn't about safety at all— it's just... autopilot.

Here's a fun experiment: get into an elevator and face the back wall. Nothing illegal. Nothing dangerous. But wow, it feels weird, doesn't it? There is no reason you have to face forward in an elevator— and yet most of us would rather die than be the one person facing the wrong direction making eye contact with strangers. That's a societal norm. A small conformity. And we follow it because we're conditioned to. Same thing with "everyone has their seat." At the boardroom table. At a weekly meeting. At the dinner table. People get attached to their spot like it's assigned by law. Sit in the wrong chair and it's like you drowned someone's cat. Those are surface conformities. And some are harmless (even funny) but they're worth noticing because they show you how often you're living by default.

Deep conformity is different. Deep conformity is when the conformity doesn't just shape your behavior— it starts shaping your belief system. It becomes internalized. It becomes identity. That's the kind that costs you. Deep conformity shows up in environments where belonging feels conditional: work, family dynamics, relationships, community spaces, even friend groups.

It looks like: staying quiet to keep the peace, swallowing the truth because it feels like "too much", muting parts of yourself so you don't get labeled, letting other people's comfort become your responsibility. You get the idea. And over time, those choices stop feeling like choices. They become your normal.

We learn about our belief systems early— often between ages four and seven— and then we spend the rest of our lives having those beliefs reinforced by family, community, and culture. Then adulthood arrives, and we start having our own thoughts… and our egos jump right in with their favorite job: keeping us "right." So, we look for proof. We fall into confirmation bias. We build echo chambers. We find ten things that validate what we already believe and ignore the hundred that challenge it. And slowly, quietly, your worldview becomes a closed loop.

So if you're feeling discomfort— that feeling of something rubbing you the wrong way— it may not be because you're broken. It may be because you've been doing the care and feeding of a belief system that no longer fits the woman you're becoming. Eventually, you'll hit a crossroads. You'll be in a moment . . . at work, in your family, in your relationship, in your community — where you know what you really think, what you really feel, what you really want to say…and you pause.

Because you don't want to make it awkward.
You don't want to be "dramatic."
You don't want to rock the boat.
You don't want to deal with the fallout.

That's your critter brain talking. The part of you wired for survival and belonging. And listen, she means well. She's been protecting you for a long time. But her volume gets loud when you're about to do something brave. And sometimes you have to treat that voice like a needy toddler: acknowledge her, thank her, and then gently send her on her way. Because the question isn't, *"Can I keep conforming?"* The question is: What is this conformity costing me?

Here's another harsh truth: as a woman, you almost can't win. If you show emotion, you're overemotional and weak. If you don't, you're cold or a bitch. If you're assertive, you're bossy. If you're agreeable, you're invisible. It's like high school: dress conservatively, you're a prude. Dress in a way that flatters your body, you're a slut. We can't win. So, at some point, you just have to own that. And if you can't win anyway, you might as well be yourself.

79

Sometimes the courage to step outside conformity isn't just for you— it becomes the permission someone else needs. I saw this in Australia during my overseas assignment. I had a boss who turned out to be a textbook sociopath. I didn't know it at first. I just thought I was asking reasonable questions and pushing back on things that felt morally wrong or business-wrong. But the moment you challenge someone like that; you become a target. The easiest thing would have been to go along so I could survive. And I tried. For a while. But then I started noticing something: people were using my office as a refuge. They'd come in shaken, confused, questioning their own sanity.

"I'm not crazy, right?"
"Didn't he say this last week?"
"Am I actually incompetent?"

And my self-protection instinct got overridden by something bigger— the instinct to help. I realized I had strengths that others didn't have in that moment, and I could either blend in… or step out. So I stepped out. It was terrifying. It was costly. And it mattered. Because sometimes being the first one to stop conforming is the thing that breaks the spell for everyone else.

The other thing I want you to remember is that transformation is usually incremental. Most of us don't have a big cinematic turning point. Change comes in small steps. Like a sapling: you can bend it way down, but it will rise again. Like a pressure cooker: the steam will build until it has to be released. Sometimes it's better to start small— to let your voice be heard in quiet ways— rather than waiting until you're so full you explode and burn everything down. The "next right step" is powerful. Because once you do the next thing, the thing after that becomes clearer. And step by step, you become the person who can do what once felt impossible.

And the discomfort you feel? It isn't proof you're doing it wrong. It's often proof you're on the edge of something new. We're wired to resist

80

change. That wiring kept our ancestors safe from saber-toothed tigers. But your nervous system never got the memo that a hard conversation isn't a predator. So, your job is to recognize the *"you might die"* response for what it is: a leftover glitch in the matrix. A signal. Not a stop sign. becomes a strange kind of reassurance. Like: *oh… here I am. I'm doing it.*

A BRAVE Breath

"You don't have to betray yourself to belong."

The Vulnerability Paradox

"What feels like exposure is often the doorway to freedom."

When I'm traveling, I have plenty of time to be alone with myself— as you can imagine. And honestly, that's not a terrible thing. I enjoy my solitude. Solitude is different from loneliness. But it *has* made me think about something: how lonely the journey of transformation can feel for so many of us. Because personal transformation is, at its core, something you walk through alone. Sure, you may have support— people who love you, mentors, coaches, friends— but at the end of the day, it's still *your* journey. Your inner work. Your truth. Your choice. And that's okay.

What makes it hard is that our ego and self-talk are loud. They chatter constantly. They convince us we're the only ones experiencing what we're experiencing. That nobody else is thinking the thoughts we're thinking. And if we let those voices run the show, we become more insular. More disconnected. We start pulling away from the people around us . . . the people who could support us, inspire us, or simply remind us: *you're not alone.*

I think it comes down to two things. First, we hide what we're going through. We hide our thoughts. We hide our doubts. We hide our mess. Second, when we *do* have thoughts that feel dark or strange or counterproductive, we panic— and push them down even harder. And that's where the paradox begins.

You've heard me say this before: because we're afraid of being vulnerable— afraid of being seen as imperfect— we create facades. We make our lives look acceptable. Sparkly. "Fine." But inside, we might be crumbling. The wild part is that we assume *everyone else* is living authentically. We think we're the only ones wearing a mask. The only ones falling behind. The only ones failing at life. Meanwhile... everyone else is doing the exact same thing. So we all walk around believing we're alone — while we're surrounded by people hiding the same things. It's a cycle we perpetuate together.

I had a moment that really drove this home. I was on a trip to Las Vegas and ended up in conversation with a man I'd met there. We were sitting, people watching, just talking— one of those unexpectedly real conversations you don't see coming. He told me about his career path. He'd gone to college, moved up in banking— teller to private banker— then moved into property management. He was making great money. Six figures. The nice home. The nice car. The partner he was "supposed" to have. On paper, he had the perfect life. And then he told me about the moment everything shifted.

He said he'd be driving to work and suddenly had flashes of thought like:

What if I swerved into oncoming traffic?

Not enough to kill him— just enough to avoid going to work. To avoid the pressure of keeping up the performance. To pause the life he was supposed to be grateful for.

He was horrified by the thought. Horrified that his mind would even go there. And I was... dumbstruck. Because I've had those thoughts too. That strange, twisted fantasy of some calamity falling into your lap ... not because you want to suffer, but because you want permission to stop pretending. Permission to escape the life that looks good but feels wrong. So, I told him: *me too.*

And something in him shifted. You could see it. That relief. That recognition. *Oh. I'm not crazy. You're not crazy. We're not alone.* That moment stayed with me. We went on to talk about the endless list of *shoulds*. The job you should have. The degree you should have. The partner you should have. The friends you should have. The car. The house. The lifestyle. These are the supposed measures of success — the ones that say you're "winning." But if we're being honest, the highest level of success isn't any of that. It's happiness. It's peace. It's contentment. And creating an environment where others can feel that, too.

And yet living for happiness is often labeled irresponsible. Self-indulgent. Frivolous. Even as I write that, you might feel the reflex: *That's not practical. There are more important things.* But are there? Look at what's happening in the world. The sadness. The anger. The pressure to keep up. To one-up. To conquer. To prove. Where is the happiness? Where is the sense of *enough*?

So why do we hide? There was an article I read years ago— I think it was in Forbes— about how people wear masks to hide their fears, wounds, and insecurities. And the problem is that after enough layers, you start losing touch with who you really are. And this is the paradox: We want validation. Recognition. Love. But to be our true selves, we risk rejection. So, we hide. But because we hide, our true selves never get validated. We end up denying the very person we want to be loved for… the right to exist. It's a game we can't win, unless we change how we play. And *this* is what conformity for comfort really is.

Except… it isn't very comfortable, is it? I've had several experiences recently where I've spoken publicly — and shared parts of my story that weren't shiny. And every time, I see the same thing in the room: That glimmer of recognition. That quiet *me too.* That moment of relief. Because there's something deeply healing about realizing you're not alone. You're not broken. You're not behind. Your thoughts aren't crazy. So yes, that guy in Vegas? He's not alone. And neither are you.

The thing is: so many people have endured job loss, heartbreak, illness, betrayal, homelessness, grief— a million forms of struggle. But most people don't talk about it. And often, all it takes is one person being brave enough to go first. Because someone out there has just a little

84

less bravery than you do — and they're waiting for a signal that it's safe to be human.

What does this mean for us? What can we actually do about it? I think there are many ways to start exercising this muscle of vulnerability. It could look like sharing part of your story in a group— a church, a professional organization, a classroom, a circle of friends. Or maybe it's not public at all. Maybe it's one person. A close friend. A sibling. A therapist. A coach. And if even that feels like too much? Start with the private version. Write it in a journal. Type it. Record a voice memo. Let the truth have a place to exist outside of your body. And if you're not even there yet, try something smaller: Practice empathy.

When you see a stranger on the street, imagine they've lived your same story. Imagine they've carried your same pain. What does that feel like? What opens inside you? It may sound odd— but your brain doesn't know the difference between real and vividly imagined. Practicing what it feels like to be seen, even in your imagination, builds capacity.

And About Those "Crazy" Thoughts... We also have to stop judging ourselves for the thoughts we have. The intrusive thoughts. The wild scenarios. The flashes of self-harm. The fantasy of someone difficult disappearing. The daydream of a miracle rescue. Yep. I said it. Because I know many of us have had those thoughts. And the goal isn't to eliminate them. The goal is to stop giving them power. Your critter brain is going to do what it does. Your ego is going to chatter. Thoughts will come. So instead of panicking... observe the thought. Acknowledge it. And let it pass. That's what meditation teaches: you don't control the thoughts— you just stop *becoming* them.

If you can begin to do two things—

1. become more visible

2. make peace with the paradox

- you'll start shifting the balance.

85

Because yes, you may risk judgment. Yes, there may be people who don't like the real you. But wouldn't it be better to let the people who only love your mask fall away... so you can create room for people who celebrate your truth? That isn't a fantasy. That's what happens. I've lived it. Every time I've taken the risk to step off the cliff of authenticity, someone showed up. Someone unexpected. Someone aligned. It's like the universe whispers: *there you are*. And once the real you appears, the life that matches her can start unfolding.

So in big ways or small ways, find your next step. Stop hiding. Stop judging your thoughts. Stop believing you're alone.

You're not crazy. You're human.

And if we stopped hiding from each other, the power of that— women living fully, honestly, visibly— would change everything.

A BRAVE Breath

"Vulnerability is not weakness — it is the bravest form of truth."

WAYPOINT FOUR — THE RECLAMATION

Where you stop outsourcing your truth— and come home to yourself.

The Reclamation is the stage where you start rebuilding your life from the inside out— but this time, on your own terms. This is where you take back your voice, your choices, your desires, your body, your time, your energy. You're no longer asking permission. You're no longer waiting for validation. You're reclaiming the parts of yourself you abandoned, ignored, or suppressed. The Reclamation is active. It's intentional. It's the stage where you stop being a passenger in your own life and start driving.

The Unintended Consequence of Facades

"The mask may protect you — but it also keeps you from being met."

There's a moment — quiet, almost imperceptible — when you realize that the one person you've never actually consulted on your own life... is you.

For most of my life, I trusted everyone else's certainty more than my own knowing...

That day, I stopped outsourcing my truth.

Self-trust doesn't require guarantees. It requires willingness. It requires presence.

This is reclamation. Not a roar, but a return. A homecoming with your own soul.

I had been living on Cape Cod for a few months (just after the COVID lockdowns started, and my separation from my husband). A group of my friends had created a Quarantine Book Club that I had been participating in. There were typically 6 or 8 of us who participated— but sometimes as few as 3 or 4. We stayed connected on weekly Zoom meetings and had an ongoing group text thread we used as sort of a stream of consciousness thing sharing bits and pieces of our lives in between our book club Zoom sessions.

One morning I was on a Zoom chat with the group – I think there were six of us that day. The conversation had meandered into non-book topics – just girlfriends chatting. One of the women had been feeling a little down. She was not very excited about her current job or her career prospects. She was also afraid to rock the boat and make a change. She mentioned that one of her fears was that she just wasn't good enough or couldn't hack it—and she would wake up most mornings with this sinking feeling that she was just faking it and would eventually get found out.

I commiserated for sure— and also said that I was exactly the same. I often felt like I was always just on the verge of veering off a cliff— that I wrestled with imposter syndrome – and often felt like I had to pretend to have my shit together so that nobody would find out.

Most of the group sort of chuckled and I heard comments like "OK. Yeah— sure Sharon— now we KNOW you are just trying to make me feel better. You are Sharon Fucking Welch – rockstar of the universe. You don't struggle with this lame shit. LOL!" etc. I did try to assure them I was not kidding or making it up – but they weren't really convinced. It wasn't a huge deal at the time and the conversation eventually moved on to other topics.

But it really stuck with me the rest of the day – it bothered me that it was so easy for them to dismiss or reject me being truly honest and vulnerable— that I had done such a good job with my façade that when I tried to come clean, I was laughed at as if I had made a joke. I wasn't really sure what to think of it.

Later that afternoon, one of the women from the group – someone who had once worked for me as an employee, and who I had also mentored for many years. She and I had become good friends over the decade we had known each other. What she said to me rocked my world. She said Sharon, I hope you don't take this the wrong way, but I was actually so relieved when you said what you said earlier on our call. For so many years I had been trying to emulate you and how you lived your life because I wanted to be the same as you – confident, successful, powerful, with all my shit together. I kept falling short and my life always seemed to have some level of mess I couldn't get rid of. It made me feel bad, and sort of embarrassed that I just couldn't get to your level. So, to hear you say that you have the same challenges that I have really hit me. I am so grateful to know that I am not necessarily a failure and that maybe my messiness and lack of confidence is sometimes normal.

Her words hit me like a gut punch. I was horrified that my well-intentioned effort to appear to have all of those things she admired (even though I was often just playing a role I thought I was supposed to play) made her feel less than and that she didn't have what it took to succeed. I had always put so much energy into maintaining my façade (across all areas of my life) so that I would be loved, accepted, envied, celebrated . . .all the things— because I thought that was the best way to help raise those around me. To hear that it actually made them feel critical of themselves for not living up to it literally brought me to tears. I have never forgotten that conversation.

I still interact with that group of women today— it has been years now. We let it all hang out and it the absolute BEST! Every single woman in that group is unique – different careers, different relationships, different bodies, different lifestyles. But when we are together it is the most supportive, fun and safe community to just be ourselves. As an example of vulnerability that we turn into fun . . .one day I was bemoaning my flabby, swingy "wings" on the underside of my arms and had made a slow-motion video of them flapping that I posted to our chat thread.

Within 10 minutes every single one of those women posted their own version of it and we are all laughing hysterically. These are the kinds of things we do all the time— we celebrate or at least poke fun of our awkwardness and flaws. And when one of us really down, the rest of us rally around for support, or tough love or a well-timed animated meme. These are the women who really taught ME about self-acceptance and true authentic grit to just be myself. I will be forever grateful!

A BRAVE Breath

*"Being seen is safer than staying hidden —
once you choose the right people."*

Feeling the Weight

"You can't heal what you keep pretending doesn't hurt."

I was reading a just-for-pleasure novel. And in the novel, the character referenced a quote from the Scarlet Letter. I was something to the effect that she didn't realize the weight until she felt the freedom. And that really hit home for me. How many times have you persevered through something or put up with something or while going through your daily life you were carrying some heavy load and you became so used to it that if it ever went away or you ever were able to address it or fix it— you felt that freedom of just shrugging off a facade or a way of being or a thought that kept bringing you down. It was probably only then that you realize the weight of what it was you had been carrying, right? It is powerful to contemplate that. She didn't realize the weight until she felt the freedom. Let that sink in.

Here is a story where I really felt that in a major way. A little personal bit about me. Several years ago, as I mentioned, I caught my husband (now ex-husband), having an online/text relationship. It definitely caused a little bit of PTSD that persisted for a number of years after that. Every time I would see him pick up his phone or a text would come in, I would tense up. It's probably a whole chapter just to talk about why I had been putting up with this for several years! But the point is that for several years, every time a text would come in, I immediately wondered, oh, is it another woman? Is it? What's happening?

I would horriblize it in my head and then I would beat myself up about it saying to myself, "Sharon— I can't believe that you're not a bigger person and that you haven't been able to forgive that and forget that and move past it. How petty that you still think that maybe it's another woman." So that had been my experience over a period of years and it

92

just became a natural part of how I was in the world. Every time that phone would ding or every time I'd see him pull his phone out of his pocket and be scrolling something, I immediately went there and after a while it just became automatic, I just didn't think about it anymore. I just had the reaction, beat myself up about it, and lather-rinse-repeat.

About a year after we separated, we ended up in the same town at a wedding for a mutual friend. We were socializing in a group of people and at one point he pulled out his phone to do something and it was like I had been hit by a Mack truck! All of a sudden, it just hit me full force in the chest and in the heart. I felt that gripping tension. I felt that weight of how I used to live. I had had an entire year of detoxing from that experience. And in one moment it all came back. By now I had been living free of that, but I certainly remembered what that weight felt like in that moment. And so when I saw this quote, she didn't realize the weight until she felt the freedom, it just really made me think about these facades we carry around – these labels.

We play these roles in our lives to be accepted, to be loved, to be appropriate, to be an adult. And some of those things weigh on us. They're not healthy. We drag around this weight. At some point it becomes so normalized. It doesn't seem so bad. It doesn't seem like a weight because we're so used to it. But isn't it interesting that the minute we let ourselves drop all that nonsense, the minute we let ourselves be authentically who we are and we feel that sense of relief— only then do we tend to realize what we've been dragging around.

So, think about that. Are there things in your life that either feel kind of meh or you find yourself wondering, is there more or is this just the way it is and it seems ok? Maybe look at that one more time and ask yourself, have you really just normalized carrying around that responsibility— carrying around that weight? And so now it just feels like the way things are, the way things have to be? Instead pause and think how do things get to be if I'm being my authentic self, if I'm really honoring myself, how do things get to be? If you start moving towards that, you will start to see just how heavy all of the other nonsense that you've been carrying around really is.

A BRAVE Breath

"Name what hurts. That is how you begin to set it down."

The Seduction of Comfort

"Comfort is easy — until it costs you your life."

So here we are. We've uncovered belief systems we didn't even realize were running in the background. We've started noticing the invisible structures we unconsciously bought into— the ones keeping us exactly where we are. We've talked about putting ourselves in situations where we can make the uncomfortable comfortable, and the unfamiliar familiar. We've talked about the pitfalls of conforming for comfort. Great. And yet... we still slide back sometimes. We fall into old habits that *vex* us. We know we want to change them, but it's so easy to go back. Which begs the question: Why are our old patterns so seductive?

This has been on my mind because it's something I've struggled with, too. I've had moments where I've had to stop, take a breath, and ask myself: *What on earth am I doing?* I've done all this work— waking up, getting out of autopilot, being intentional with the time I have left (hopefully a lot of time). I've been living this way for years. And then every once in a while, I find myself right back in an old loop. It's crazy-making. But the more I've watched it, the more I've realized: there are a few common reasons it happens.

The first one is simple: we're busy. We're juggling multiple things at once— sometimes with what looks like grace and ease, but inside it can feel overwhelming. And when life gets loud, our brains start building shortcuts wherever they can. If you've ever done any training around micro-inequities, you've heard this: human beings like to put things in boxes. We like rules of thumb. We make assumptions "as a general rule" because it's the easy button. It reduces the mental load. It's not always right. It's not always fair. But it's what the brain does to cope. And that same mechanism shows up in personal change. When we're overwhelmed, we reach for what we know. We go back to the automatic response— because it costs less energy. It requires less presence. It allows us to run on autopilot. That's why you'll notice it most when you stop doing your grounding rituals. When you fall off the wagon with the morning routine— meditation, journaling, the gym, a few breaths, whatever brings you back into your body. Not because you don't care— but because you're maxed out. So one reason you slide back into old patterns is simply this: You're overwhelmed.

The second reason is more primal. Any time you're building a new habit, it feels uncomfortable at first. Whether it's yoga, flossing, journaling, speaking up, setting boundaries— the beginning always feels awkward. And your critter brain hates awkward. We're hardwired from prehistoric times to avoid risk. Back then, unfamiliar often *was* dangerous. So your nervous system still reads unfamiliarity as: *unsafe… you might die… go back to the cave.* Of course, we're not running from lions anymore. We're not being chased by boulders. But the brain never got the memo. So sometimes you return to an old pattern because it feels safe— even if it's not the direction you actually want to go.

I was thinking about all of this the other day while I was walking along the beach. I had a lot going on— business-wise, personally— and I noticed myself falling back into old patterns. Some were physical patterns. Some were mental. Some were emotional. And instead of beating myself up, I paused and got curious: *Huh. That's interesting. Why did I fall back into that pattern?* When I looked closely, the answer was obvious. I was juggling too much. And honestly? It was kind of nice to put a few things back on autopilot. It was like slipping into comfortable pajamas. Like grabbing your favorite ice cream and watching a rom-com. Familiar. Easy. Comforting.

But that comfort has a cost. Because when I go on autopilot, I stop being present. And when I stop being present, I start defaulting to the old version of me— the one I'm actively outgrowing. So I did what I always do when I catch myself: I took a few breaths. I didn't shame myself. I didn't dramatize it. I just asked: *What's the root cause?* And for me, the root cause was overwhelm— and a lapse in my grounding practices.

Here's another truth: your critter brain is... kind of dumb. I say that lovingly. It doesn't know what's true versus imagined. It doesn't know what's happening now versus what happened five years ago. It doesn't know the difference between the past, the future, and the story you're spiraling in at 2 a.m. That's why visualization works. That's why role play works. That's why imagining your "perfect day" can shift your physiology. Your brain responds to what you *feed* it. So when you notice yourself back in an old pattern, sometimes the move is simple: Pause. Tell yourself something different. Move forward again. That's it. No massive drama required.

Even with all the work I've done, I still have those half-steps backward sometimes. And you will too. The key is not to turn it into proof that you're broken. Don't add it to your internal list of self-criticism and demoralization. Because if you keep returning to what's familiar just because it's familiar, you make growth impossible.

I was watching the Sex and the City follow-on series, *And Just Like That*— where the characters are in their fifties navigating reinvention (which feels... incredibly on brand for my life right now). And there's a line that hit me:

"It's better to be confused than to be sure, because when you're sure, nothing can change."

How often do we feel shame when we're unsure? How often do we hide confusion— and fear— like it's some kind of weakness? But confusion and discomfort are often the threshold of growth. And I love this little reminder: In the word *discomfort*, the first three letters mean *do it still*. Those "go back to the cave" voices? The ones that want comfort at any cost? Think of them like nagging kids. Most of the time they just want attention. So you can acknowledge them without obeying them: "Thank you. You kept me safe for a long time. But I don't need that kind of support right now. I've got this." And the only way to make something unfamiliar become familiar is to keep doing it. Even if you step back half a step, then step forward again— you're still doing it. And at some point, the new patterns become the comfortable ones... and the old patterns start to fall away.

Now, we can know all of this and still struggle. And most of the time when it feels *stuck-stuck*— not just a temporary slide— it circles back to beliefs we haven't examined yet. Because beliefs are the core operating system. They shape how we spend money. How we choose relationships. How we work. How we rest. How we treat ourselves. What we reach for when we're scared. When you haven't rooted out a few limiting beliefs, the pressure builds. You feel tense. You feel dissonance. And then you fall back into the old patterns because they require less inner negotiation. So yes: sometimes the reason you keep returning to the same habit isn't lack of discipline. It's a belief you haven't named yet.

There are four I see over and over:

1. **"I'm not good enough."**
   Possibly the most damaging belief on the planet— and it's everywhere now because we're constantly comparing ourselves to curated narratives. It's a lie that keeps you small.

2. **"It's possible for them, but not for me."**
   This one hides in "circumstances." It convinces you that other people have got the opportunities, support, money, energy, confidence— and you don't. But the real issue isn't circumstances. It's the belief you're powerless.

3. **"I just need to fix one more thing before I'm ready."**
   A beautifully disguised avoidance tactic. A checklist you never finish. A moving finish line.

4. **"I have no time."**

   This one is dangerous because it becomes the game you keep winning. And remember: we are wired to win.

So, choose the right tournament. Because if you play the game of "I don't have time," you'll win that game. If you play the game of "I'm not enough," you'll win that game too. So, the question becomes: what game are you choosing?

If you're noticing an old belief running the show, here's a process:

- Ask: **Is it actually true?**

- Identify: **Where did I get this belief?**

- Declare: **I don't believe this anymore.**

- Find proof: **Collect evidence it isn't true.**

- Replace it: **Choose a new belief as the antidote.**

- Prove the new one: **Collect evidence until it feels real.**

- Test it: **Observe how you feel, act, and what results you create.**

Your ego wants to prove you right. So, give it a new assignment.

Are you starting to see how all of this is tied together? Beliefs. Autopilot. The seduction of comfort. The voice that wants safety. The patterns that return when you're overwhelmed. It's not simple— and it gets more complicated as we age, because we have more responsibility, more input, more pressure, and more tentacles in the world. But you still must start somewhere. You still have to take the next step. And the good news is: you are already winning. You're always winning— at the game you're playing. So just be careful which tournament you've entered.

Are you competing in:

- "I never have enough time"

- "I always choose wrong"

- "I don't deserve this"

- "I'll do it when I'm ready"

Or are you competing in:

- "I always have time for what matters"

- "I am allowed to evolve"

- "I deserve love and respect"

- "I can do the next brave thing"

Because those are trophies too. And if the games you're winning are keeping you small… it might be time to up your game.

A BRAVE Breath

"Comfort can be a pause — but it can't be your forever."

Meaning or Purpose?

"Purpose isn't found — it's remembered."

One morning, I was doing something that I typically do. Part of my morning routine is to read something, listen to something, experience something where I can learn something new or gain a new perspective or grow in some way as a human being. So this particular morning, I happened to read an article about seven aspects or qualities it takes to be a good leader— not the typical, you know, cherry lollipop ones that you see, but the ones that are less talked about— the ones that are less glamorous— the ones that are kind of down in the trenches. Let's come back to that in a minute.

Then the other thing was I listened to a podcast with a PhD from Cornell University who was talking about the difference between meaning and purpose in our lives. She was talking about how easy it is to get those confused and what that might look like. Then it morphed into this conversation about the relationship between goals and purpose, which are two things that are related, but again, not interchangeable and not the same thing. The beginning of the conversation was about how many times— as we go to seek meaning in our lives— that requires us to look backwards. We have to look back, analyze, catalog, categorize things that have or have not happened to us— things that we have acquired or not acquired. We do this all the time as we go through life. And if we look back, that is really how we are trying to assign meaning.

Trying to find meaning is really an exercise in looking back. Whereas purpose is always in front of us. Our purpose is constantly renewing and revealing infinite pathways for how we are to show up and contribute in the world. Now you've often heard me say, it's the difference between who you are being as opposed to what you were

101

doing. Your purpose is really about who you were going to be in the world and that will naturally come out of some things that you will do. But you've got to understand who you're being first.

So, it was in this conversation with this PhD where I better understood this idea of purpose being quite different from meaning. We can assign all sorts of meaning to things. and it's a largely personal exercise or an exercise that is conditioned through how we were raised or the societal constraints that we live in. That's how we define and measure meaning in something. Purpose is a purely internal and personal exercise of who you want to be in the world. What lights you up, what brings you joy or contentedness or feelings of abundance or feelings of belonging— all of these things that as humans we want to have.

That was a great perspective on that, which led to where do goals play into that. We hear plenty of others— particularly like the hard-hitting business coaches— who talk about how you've got to have this five-year plan, you've got to set these goals and when you knock out these goals, again, we've created another measurement about whether we are a good or bad, successful or a failure. We are trying to measure if we are doing it right— did we meet these goals. You may then wonder why it is sometimes when you achieve those goals, you knock the hell out of your five-year plan, you're going on all cylinders and you get to the other side of that achievement and invariably you find yourself wondering one of two things. Either is that it or what's next? Right?

So, while those thoughts of what's next or is that it can propel you forward, oftentimes it's in that space where we have those feelings of maybe floating or disconnectedness, disappointment, disillusionment, depression and anxiety. When you go charging at these goals and you achieve them and you wonder why you still maybe feel empty or not complete or broken. Now I use the term broken tentatively— as there is nobody who's broken, there's no such thing as being broken. There are just things you don't understand yet or that people don't understand about you. But I'm using that term because I know we have feelings of that sometimes.

But then why are we making goals? Are they even important? Yes, they are. But they need to be in the context of your purpose. I always say, change your mind, change your life and that it's who you are and your belief system that sets in motion how you show up in the world, the habits that you have, the actions that you take, the ways that you think about things. So, it stands to reason that until you understand your purpose, there is no container or roadmap for your goals. Think about that. You can set goals all day long, you can set New Year's resolutions if you want.

But if they are at odds with who you are, your identity, your belief system, if they are at odds with your purpose, you can probably achieve those goals – no doubt. I know you can, I know all of you are motivated. You are strong people. I get that. But those goals aren't necessarily going to feed you. Those goals aren't necessarily going to put you in a mindset of feeling that you have a contented, joyful, abundant life if they're not tied to your purpose. And more than likely, they are going to exhaust you with the constant care and feeding required to maintain them.

This is just another way of saying what I've always said, that to really change how your life is going, to really change that trajectory, you have to really be willing to uncover and visit your belief system. And for a lot of us, this belief system, as I've said many times, is something that's handed to us when we're very young and impressionable. And then, it's reinforced in our family of origin in our communities, in our societies. As we get older and we have that ability to critically reason, then as humans, we want to be right? So, confirmation bias comes into play where then we want to feel reassured that we're right, that we are doing things right, that we are ok and acceptable in the world. So, we will go find indications that our belief system is right from an external perspective. The real work of finding your purpose, the real work of living out loud is to question every single one of those beliefs and that takes courage. It takes vulnerability. It takes resilience.

You're seeing a pattern here in the Journey to BRAVE— bold, resilient, authentic, vulnerable, evolving. That is the journey you must go on to look at these beliefs and then decide for yourself if the belief is true for you still. Has it ever been true for you? Why or why not? How does it show up in your life? If it's not true for you, what is a belief that is more true for you? And how can you start embodying that new belief? It's only when you peel back that onion and get down to that and figure out what truly you believe in that you can go forward authentically from there.

Not when everyone else told you, you gotta believe it, not what everybody else told you was right or acceptable, what you believe. It's a very personal journey. Then who you are being truly is in resonance with your purpose, which means those beliefs are going to lead to your habits and actions that embody that new belief system, that new identity. Pretty powerful, right? But I'm telling you, this is how it all works.

So that first step is really being willing to have those conversations. All of those goals that you want to set are great. They're great steps along the path to your purpose. You never reach the end of the line for your purpose. Your purpose continues to infinitely unfold in front of you as you go through a life, a life that is off of autopilot, a life that you are fully engaged in. That evolving purpose never goes away. You never get to the end of the road of that purpose because if you did think about what that means— life's done! So, let's hope we all live to really, really old ages— the whole time feeling cared for and abundant and content and loved and accepted by just being ourselves.

Now, coming back to this article that I read after hearing this conversation. One of the things that stood out to me in this article was the idea that you have to know yourself before you can grow yourself, which also means as a leader, you must know everything about yourself, warts and all before you can be better. But then you also must know the people around you that you are in service to before you can help them grow as well. Something to think about in your own journey— you must know yourself before you can grow yourself. This journey is figuring out who you really are and what is the belief system that works for you. And then you must ask, what does that mean to show up in the world to fulfill that purpose?

Another aspect of that is if you are walking alongside someone on a journey or if you are trying to help someone in their journey, you can't do that from your roadmap. Your roadmap only belongs to you. The same is true for the support and help you get for yourself— no coach, no advisor, no confidant, no partner can help you with your journey from their own map. The people who can truly help you are the ones who can get on *your* map and try to understand your map. And if that's not happening for you in the support relationships you have, then those aren't the people to help you on your journey. They're just not. They may be great. Maybe they're cool to hang out with, maybe they're even great to be married to, but they're not going to be the people who ultimately can help you with your journey.

You have to be known to be able to be helped to grow just like you have to know yourself to be able to grow yourself. Just think about that as you're on this journey. This is a critical message for you— that it's about who you're being not what you're doing. And the only way to know who you're being or who you want to be is to really understand and get down to what your purpose is. What is that thing that makes you, that helps you to feel fulfilled. And then that journey and that understanding is what allows you to grow. And people being willing to learn about your map is how they can help you get there, not you fitting into someone else's map.

A BRAVE Breath

"Follow the thread of what makes you feel alive."

WAYPOINT FIVE — THE INTEGRATION

Where the becoming shows up quietly— and you choose it anyway.

The Integration is the stage where your new way of being becomes your normal. The practices you've been working on— boundaries, authenticity, intuition, self-trust— are no longer effortful experiments. They're just how you live now. You've moved from consciously choosing yourself to unconsciously embodying yourself. The Integration is where transformation settles into your bones. Where the new you isn't new anymore— she's just you.

Don't Make it Special

"Your 'ordinary' story is enough to change everything."

Integration is sneaky.

We imagine transformation as fireworks— a lightning bolt, a breakthrough, an Oprah-worthy moment. But the truth is far softer. Integration shows up in the ordinary. Each small, aligned action is a vote for your future self. You didn't become someone new. You stopped abandoning who you were all along.

Prior to leaving on a long winter trip, I did a multi-day juice cleanse. It was not necessarily for any particular reason, but I just wanted to try it. I'm curious about all sorts of things. So I decided to do this cleans. Now while that experience is a whole another story in and of itself, having had some pretty terrible moments there as my system got rid of a number of things that I'm sure were polluting my liver and kidneys! But one of the outcomes was I was able to really detox needing the level of caffeine in my life that I had built up to having. Since that time, I have been drinking little to no caffeine. Fast forward to my trip to Central America. Now, as you can imagine in that part of the world, (which is like where all the coffee comes from!) coffee is a major thing! Decaf coffee is *not* at thing.

I love coffee and prior to the cleanse— I was filling my body with caffeine religiously every single day. Not just coffee in the morning, but I also always had unsweetened iced tea in my refrigerator. It was a staple. I probably drank more of that than I drank water or anything else. So now post cleanse— I was curious how that was going to play out on this trip. I had actually been counting how many days, how many weeks, how many months it had been since I'd had any caffeine. And then this one morning, I was having breakfast at the cafe of a new friend who I met in Nicaragua. We were just chatting amiably, and I was watching him prepare orders for other people who were at this little cafe that he owned. Then he starts making a coffee, drink— a really strong coffee in a traditional Moka pot— which I first became aware of when I was in Europe.

I looked at him and I said, wow, you know, oh, man, boy, do I miss coffee! It's been, I don't know, 43.5 days or whatever I said for how long it had been. He sort of chuckled and he said, you know, something to think about though is when you turn the deprivation of something into a competition and/or into something that you're measuring by hours or days or weeks, you really feel that sense of deprivation and likely because of feeling that loss, even if you don't go back to the thing, you will likely just replace it with something else so that you don't feel the loss because you've made it special. And I just looked at him and I was like, my friend, my guru! This is just not the way that I had thought about things, but he was right.

There are so many times that it's not that we're intending to deprive ourselves of things in our life. Maybe it's not caffeine or food— maybe it's not something that visceral— but maybe we're deciding that we need to have less social media or we need to sit around less or . . .there's a million different things that we try to take away from our lives and it's very well meaning. But the way that we do it tends to come from a place of scarcity. And we make those things special. So, by losing it, by not having it, we focus on it. And when we focus on it, it feels kind of icky and it feels like this challenge and it feels like this competition for how long we can withstand depriving ourselves of this thing that we've made special.

It was just such a good reminder that whatever those things are that you are cutting out of your life— It could be toxic people. It could be an environment that just doesn't feel healthy and nourishing and supportive of you and who you are. It could be anything. It doesn't have to be caffeine. When we make it special and when we start patting ourselves on the back for how long we've been able to power through withholding that from ourselves, it just makes it all the harder to really let it go and we will artificially fill it with something that's maybe just as bad, if not worse so that we can feel that comfort – or so we don't have to feel that discomfort of losing or being deprived of that thing. Whereas if we didn't make it special and we just released it, the discomfort would never take root. What we've really made room for is for that void to be filled with something that comes to us naturally, that flows to us. We now have room for something that's nourishing for us physically, mentally, emotionally, spiritually, just something to think about while you're sipping your morning coffee.

A BRAVE Breath

"The challenges grown more impossible when you make them special."

Rest is the Secret Sauce

"Rest isn't a reward — it's a requirement."

Maybe you've heard about the importance of rest and integration after a season of big growth— a big "muscle movement" in your life. I've learned this one the personal way. I spent four months traveling through Central America one winter. Part of that was practical: one part of my business slows down in winter— the location-dependent part— so I had some freedom to travel. But it was also something deeper. Central America speaks to me. Honestly, it's probably a place I'll settle someday. And I wanted to *feel* it— not just visit it.

I traveled through different countries, spending about a month at a time in each place. I was giving myself space away from my normal patterns and systems so I could question things: my beliefs, my life stories, my inner dialogue, the scripts I run without realizing it. And yes… I did a lot of growing on that trip. Then I landed somewhere unexpected. At one point I ended up in San Isidro de Grecia, in the Central Valley of Costa Rica— far from the beaches where you'd normally find me. When I arrived at my Airbnb, I was a little alarmed. It was *way* more rural than I expected. I had a mini internal panic: this was going to be logistically complicated. Getting to a restaurant, a shop, a grocery store— everything felt like it would take effort.

But after a few days, I realized something: It was exactly what I needed. It was quiet. Peaceful. No constant sense of "I should be out doing something." No tourist pressure. No FOMO. No compulsion to prove I was "making the most of it." The universe knew. So, there I was— getting comfortable with just… *being*.

We get this messaging that if you're not growing, you're dying. If you're not moving forward, you're falling behind. If you're not climbing, then you're irrelevant. So, we keep pushing toward the next thing and the next thing and the next thing. But constant forward motion has a cost. Because it prevents us from experiencing what's right here. Yes, growth matters. We should keep evolving our whole lives. And also— we need time for growth to *take root*. We need time for it to become part of who we are. To integrate into how we show up in the world. That can't happen when we're always sprinting.

We need stillness. Quiet. Space to reflect. Space to let the lesson settle into our bones. And here's the kicker: stillness can be uncomfortable. Because when you're still, you can hear yourself. That's when you have to look in the mirror. That's when the thoughts show up— the ones questioning your value, your choices, your sanity, your *worthiness*. It can feel uncomfortable to rest. And that's exactly why so many of us don't. But when we refuse to rest, growth can become just another form of numbing. You can numb with work. You can numb with busy-ness. You can numb with food, alcohol, shopping, scrolling, achievement, productivity. There are a million ways to avoid the "icky" parts— the uncomfortable parts— the parts we'd rather not feel. But when you numb out the hard stuff, you also numb out the good. You numb out love. Joy. Gratitude. Presence. The beauty and abundance that are actually right in front of you. So, when we're forced into quiet— or when we finally choose it— it can cause panic at first. But it's also where integration happens.

Look at the plant world. Plants do most of their big growth in spring. Then there's a period where they stop growing... and they bear fruit. The fruit is the outcome of the growth. It's what becomes possible *because* the growth happened. We're the same. When you take on a new job, finish a degree, complete a retreat, go through a major life shift— you don't just need the growth. You need the pause afterward. You need the breath. You need time to digest what you just became.

A perfect example for me was that winter trip. I knew I'd be moving from place to place, but I also had long stretches— a month at a time— to actually soak in the community. Except for January. In January, I was in six different places. Yes, self-inflicted. There was a retreat in Mexico, and the logistics around it were complicated. I bounced around more than I planned. And here's what I didn't realize at the time: I was doing an enormous amount of internal work at that retreat. The kind that cracks you open. Radical authenticity. Vulnerability. Deep relating. The kind of space where you look at it all, reorganize it, and rebuild it bigger and truer. You come out of something like that raw. And you need integration.

But when I left the retreat, I went to Mexico City— a busy, chaotic place. Not exactly ideal for "soft landings." The universe gave me a boost that didn't feel like a gift at the time: I caught a chest cold. So, I wasn't out conquering the city, but I still wasn't really resting. Then I moved on to Panama— also in a big-city environment. Again, not recognizing how much space I truly needed. A few weeks after that spiritual muscle movement, I hit a dip. I felt lost. A little depressed. I started questioning everything. The critter brain came out with a megaphone:

Do you even know how to do adulting?
Do you make good decisions?
Can you really live the life you say you want?

All the gremlins showed up. And for one of the first times ever, I did something that is notoriously hard for recovering superwomen: I reached out to my tribe for help. I asked for support. And it shouldn't surprise you what happened next: people showed up. Not just to support me, but to say, *me too*. They could empathize. They'd been there— either right then, or before. It reinforced a theme I keep seeing everywhere: We need to stop hiding from each other. Because so much of this human experience is shared— and we're not meant to carry it alone.

After that month in the city, I thought I was ready to get back to it. Like, okay— I've had my retreat, I've had some time, now let's go explore more places in Costa Rica I might want to live. And then I arrived in San Isidro de Grecia. Coffee plantations. Sugar cane farms. Dirt roads. Quiet so deep it feels like a physical weight on your ears. At first, I was freaked out. But within days, I recognized it: This was the integration I needed. No distractions. No tourist checklist. No noise. Just me— and everything I'd learned— with enough space for it to land. I could sit with the good and the uncomfortable. Let the feelings have their moment. Figure out what belonged in my life… and what didn't. It was an accidental gift.

And it is connected to something else I've learned about myself: in Human Design terms, I have a sacral authority. (If you've never heard of Human Design, it's one of many tools that can offer insight into how you're wired.) For me, the best decisions come from my gut— my true gut. Not the gut I've litigated. Not the gut I've Googled. The gut that responds with a visceral *hell yes* or *hell no*. And here's what I've noticed: right after an intense experience— a retreat, a breakthrough, a big emotional moment— everything looks enticing. You're on a high. You want the next thing and the next thing and the next thing. I had plenty of that swirling around me: projects, ideas, trips, offerings, things to write, things to record, things to build. And my gut response wasn't a clean yes. It was more like: *maybe… yes… but not yet.* There was a "yes," but I couldn't hear what came after it. And it wasn't until I got distance from the excitement— until I was in a quieter place— that I finally heard the rest of the sentence:

That's the part we miss when we never stop moving. And what I keep learning is this: once you start waking up to your patterns, you can't unsee them. Once you start listening to your inner voice, you can hear more than you ever could before. So, when you get that quiet nudge— that surprising "try this," that unexpected "pause here," that gentle redirection— have the courage to follow it, at least for a little while.

Nothing is permanent. You can always change your mind. But if you never explore the road that keeps calling you, you might miss the turning point that changes everything.

That month of rural quiet helped me uncover rhythms I want to preserve: how I wake up, how I go to sleep, how I move my body, how I feed myself, how I interact with people, how I live inside my own days. I wanted to take those things back with me. Not because I believed life would become a rainbow unicorn Pollyanna miracle when I returned— it won't. Real life is real life. But the truth is: regular life can drown out what matters if you're not present. Mindfulness matters. Presence matters. Integration matters. And it looks different for everyone— there's no "right" way.

Let me ask you this: Have you ever had a major breakthrough— a huge growth moment— and your next thought was immediately, *Okay... what's next?* The thing is: there will always be something next. You don't have to worry about that. The next thing is coming whether you chase it or not. So please— let yourself enjoy this moment. Celebrate this mountain you just climbed. Let it sink into you. Let it become part of who you are. And then, when the next growth moment comes— before you rush off to conquer the next mountain— I hope you remember:

Rest is not wasted time. It's where the growth becomes *yours*.

A BRAVE Breath

"Rest is not quitting. Rest is listening."

Reintegrating the Extraordinary
Into the Typical

"Becoming whole is learning to hold all of you."

I had recently returned to the U.S. after several months of traveling overseas— and I was suddenly face-to-face with the reintegration process. And it struck me how what we assume is "normal forever and ever amen" is really just… what we're used to. Coming back to my old routines— the places I live, the things I eat, the people I interact with— all of it felt strangely foreign. And it was wild to realize that just four or five months earlier, *this* was my norm.

I've been reflecting a lot on that winter journey: what I learned, what I practiced, what challenged me, and what changed me— including the ways I was *forced* into seeing things from a different perspective. Because sometimes it's hard to shift perspective when you're inside your comfort zone. It's so easy to live on autopilot. And to be fair— autopilot *can* be self-preservation.

Autopilot helps us process the boring day-to-day input without having to consciously think about every single detail. But there are pitfalls to it. And one of those pitfalls is how quickly we fall back into old patterns— especially after we've stretched ourselves into something new. I've been thinking about that a lot since coming home.

Because when you push yourself out of your comfort zone, and you *don't* rest, integrate, and allow your growth to become your natural way of being… it's so easy to slip back into what you know. It's just easier. Familiar. Automatic. And I'm noticing this will probably be challenging for me. There were ways of being I developed while traveling that I want to maintain now that I'm back. I was more connected to nature. I ate differently. I slept differently. I moved through life more slowly . . . paying attention, noticing small miracles. All of those things felt natural overseas.

And now, back in the U.S., I can feel how quickly that gets derailed. I say "typical" on purpose, because I don't love the word normal. I think "normal" is a limiting term— and honestly, a misleading one. A lot of times, normal just means what we're used to. Think about how many things in your daily life get labeled "not normal" simply because they don't match what you expect— even if they're completely fine. Normal is subjective. Fluid. Flexible. It changes with your experience. So, my return to the U.S. was really a return to the life I've *typically* lived in the past. And it's been uncomfortable at times to integrate what I want to preserve from overseas. Those discoveries— those shifts— happened because I was in an environment that made space for them. Space to notice. Space to breathe. Space to expand. Back in a completely different world— physically, emotionally, ideologically— they don't fit quite as easily. I've been coming up against challenges in continuing those practices that felt so natural abroad. And I think this is what happens on our inner journey too.

We have an awakening... an insight... an "aha." We discover something new about ourselves, or we take a chance, or we build a new part of ourselves that feels more authentic.

And then we try to take off the training wheels and live that truth in the typical world... and suddenly it feels hard. Or worse— it feels like maybe we're wrong. Maybe we imagined it. Maybe there's no room for this version of us. But I think this struggle is normal— and the trip reminded me of that in a physical, visceral way. I could literally *watch* it unfold as I moved from an unfamiliar world back into my familiar one. And I realized it's so similar to rediscovering yourself on the inside... and then trying to express that self on the outside.

Another thing I've been observing since coming home is how stress, anxiety, and uncertainty physically show up in my body. During my travels, I had the space to really be in my body. I did yoga. Breathwork. Meditation. I spent time alone in nature. I had stillness— and because of that, I started noticing things about myself I had never fully seen before. One of the biggest? When I'm stressed, I hold my breath. Not metaphorically— literally.

And I know this is common. We're constantly told, "Come back to the breath." But it was eye-opening to realize I actually go into a mini trance of holding my breath when I'm under stress— to the point that when I finally snap out of it, I'm out of breath and have to gulp air to recalibrate. The more mindful I became on the trip, the more I caught myself doing it. And over time, I started doing it less. I began breathing *into* discomfort instead of bracing against it. Then I came back home. I started driving again— something I hadn't done in months— and immediately noticed myself holding my breath again. But this time, I caught it faster… because I'd learned what it felt like to *not* do it. And that made me wonder: Do you deprive yourself of your own breath just to get through something? If you do, it might be time to remember some of the quick tools in your pack: pause… exhale… release… return.

Another huge realization I made— one that honestly still blows my mind— was about the way stress has lived in my body for *years*. For a long time, I carried excess weight. And in hindsight, I can see that it was a kind of force field. A protective barrier. It insulated me from a world I didn't feel safe in. I didn't feel good about myself. I didn't feel worthy. So my body created protection in the most literal way possible. That part wasn't entirely new to me.

But wait… there was more.

One thing I had always prided myself on was my rock-hard abs. No, really. I used to joke that it must be genetics— because even when I carried extra weight, my abs were still strong. Until this winter. Because as I started doing embodiment work— learning to truly relax my body— I realized something startling: My abs were "rock hard" because my gut was always clenched. I had been walking through most of my adult life braced for a gut punch. Let that sink in.

It was only when I learned to systematically relax that I even noticed the clench. And when I felt it release… it was emotional. Like my body was finally exhaling a decades-long survival strategy. That moment wasn't about turning something "positive" into a negative. It was about realizing my body had been protecting me for years— because I wasn't mentally and emotionally ready to do it for myself. And now I am. To feel that clench, and then release it on purpose, was one of the most powerful moments of my trip. My body gave me the signal: you don't need armor anymore.

I also had new experiences while traveling— like feeling blue. Feeling sad. Feeling out of sorts. Even feeling a little depressed sometimes. And then… feeling guilt about it. Because if you're doing something other people dream about, you automatically take on this invisible list of expectations. You're supposed to be grateful every moment. Sparkly. Inspired. Alive. And when you're not, you feel like you've failed at the experience. I had off days where I wanted to stay in bed, cry, read, rest. I had moments of FOMO about what was happening back home. I made connections with people and then had to detach and move on— which is its own form of emotional labor.

And then the voice would come in: *How dare you feel sad? You're in paradise.* It's ridiculous. And yet… so common. And then there was the other side of it. Sometimes I just wanted to sit in a hammock and read a book— not because I was sad, but because it felt nourishing. And still, the critter brain would say: *But you're in a place with 20 bucket list activities! Go go go! Don't waste the opportunity!* That pressure is everywhere. And what I learned is this: How you travel, how you create, how you live— it's all personal. The only expectations worth meeting are your own. And even those need to be questioned, because often they're built on "should." And *should* is almost never your agenda. It's somebody else's.

So, I started practicing something radical: Doing nothing without guilt. Rest as a ritual. Because doing nothing is still something. Sometimes rest is integration. Sometimes it's just sitting in a chair and listening to birdsong. No productivity. No proof. No measurable output. And those moments are just as important as anything on the bucket list.

I also realized something else that applies far beyond travel: You don't need to cram every possible experience into one life chapter. It's like eating until you're full... not until you clean your plate. Because when you try to do everything, you spread yourself thin and create a mediocre version of a hundred things— instead of a rich, full, present experience of the few that matter most. And when you do that, you don't feel satiated. You feel hungry. Because you're always chasing the next thing and the next thing and the next thing. But when you slow down and savor what's right in front of you, something magical happens: The phantom hunger starts to fade. The pressure to keep pursuing melts away. And what's truly important becomes clear.

One of my biggest takeaways from traveling is this: Even the things you forget are still working inside you. Just because you didn't document it doesn't mean it didn't happen. Just because you can't recall it perfectly doesn't mean it didn't change you. We do this all the time— this anxious compulsion to capture everything. How many times have you taken a course, worked with a coach, learned a skill, had a profound insight... and panicked that if you can't recite it later, it doesn't count? But the truth is: your subconscious doesn't forget. This is why trauma still shapes us even when we "forgot" it— because it's still running in the background. And the same is true for healing. For growth. For the positive inputs. Even if you forget the exact words or steps, those things become part of how you move through the world. You find yourself doing something and realize: *Oh... I learned this. I forgot I learned this.* That's why I love the way my Spanish audio course is taught— the instructor literally says not to take notes. He expects you to forget. He encourages it. Because forgetting is part of learning. And part of integration. And he's right.

So this is what I'm reminding myself as I reintegrate back into my typical world: I don't have to remember everything for some script for a made-for-Lifetime movie. The growth is still in me. And it will rise when I need it.

Change doesn't happen on a schedule— not mine, not yours, not anyone else's. It filters through layers: personal layers, community layers, ancestral layers. It takes time. Some things stick. Some things fade. Some things return later as a surprise. The only thing we can do is keep stretching. Keep asking questions. Keep being open. Keep allowing ourselves to be vulnerable— with other people, with the world, and with ourselves. And you don't need a four-month journey overseas to do that. It's available everywhere— in your commute, at your job, at your kid's soccer game, at happy hour, in the grocery store. The extraordinary is always present. But integration... happens on its own timeline. And more often than not, you'll be delighted when you notice the growth show up again— quietly, naturally— like it was always there.

A BRAVE Breath

"Wholeness is not perfection — it's presence."

The Now and the Not Yet

"Growth lives in the in-between—
where you're brave enough to keep going."

I want to do something a little bit different for this chapter. I want to share an experience that I wrote about in real time, as opposed to after the fact.

Obviously, the experience is now in fact "after the fact" – but that can't be helped when writing a book. So instead, I will share what I wrote and was thinking at the time I was going through the experience rather than giving you the polished download at the end. I think that many times coaches, mentors, leaders— even our friends and family sometimes— will wait until they've seen the outcome. They will wait till they've seen the verdict of some challenge that they've gone through.

They'll wait till the shiny recovery to tell the story. And I think that's natural. I think it's certainly true for people who are in positions where people are watching them or where people have expectations of them, real or perceived. There tends to be a level of pressure that we put on ourselves to be the example, to be the inspiration— even though we are human, just like everyone else. And so that being said, following is an example of that, written in real time while I was going through it.

What I wanted to do today is to be vulnerable and be a little uncomfortable and talk about an experience that I'm having in real time and what I'm doing to work through it. I'm definitely not through to the other side yet. . . There was a song— it had to have been in the 80s— that had some lyrics that said something to the effect that "I'm caught in between the now and the not yet. No longer what we were before, but not all that we will be." And I am in that place right now. Over the last couple of weeks, I've been in this sort of doldrums after a period where I had this burst of energy for several months.

It was a really creative period for me, launching this podcast and starting to write a book and trying to build up some parts of my business and to reach out and develop deep connections and friendships with people that I've been meeting along the way. And I got to a point in the last couple of weeks where I'm sitting here holding my breath, waiting for everything to take root. I see exactly where I want to be and I know the things that I want to do, and they haven't all manifested yet. So I really am caught in between the now and the not yet, and it can feel at times like it's just never going to come.

Now there's this bizarre void space in there where I'm not who I used to be and also I'm not who I'm going to be. In the meantime, I struggle to hang on to my identity and just trust that the process takes the time that it takes. Seeds that you plant will germinate at some point and bear fruit, but we don't get to control where that happens or when that happens. And that's the place that I've been in and when I'm in those periods of the waiting and those periods of the doubting, that's when all of the ego talk, all of the negative self-talk, tends to rear its ugly head.

You get into this sort of echo chamber that would have you believe that clearly since everything has not unfolded in front of you the way that you envisioned and the way that you worked so hard or invested time and energy into, that surely you must be a failure. Those voices are really, really loud. This is the place that I sit in. Waiting for those seeds that you've planted to sprout and bear fruit can be scary, frustrating, and demoralizing. It's really easy to go into a bit of feeling sorry for oneself. It's really easy to horribleize everything.

It's really easy to play the game of thinking you know that this now means that this other thing is going to happen that was less desirable in your life. And it feels really true. It feels like you're a failure. I right now feel like I'm a failure. I feel misunderstood. I feel like I maybe don't know what I'm doing. I question my ability to adult. What I've been doing the last couple weeks is letting myself have the emotions. There is nothing wrong with any emotion. They are not good or bad.

123

They're there to feel them. They are an indicator of something to you. I've been allowing myself to feel the emotions without judgement.

But also being careful and mindful that I'm not wallowing in those emotions. I am trying my hardest to not let those noisy, negative voices throw me off track. I'm trying my hardest to find something every day that I can think about that's different from that, and sometimes it works and sometimes it doesn't. Even when I go through these periods. I don't find my way out perfectly. It's very easy to be on the outside. It's very easy to be the mirror for someone and tell them what they should do, what they could do, what's going to work. And it's all delivered with really good intention in a perfectly put together package.

But we all know, because we've all been in those places where we're trying to come out the other side, that it's never that cut and dried, and nobody's perfect at it. It's humbling to be reminded of that, and to go through something like that myself again. In my own journey over the last several years, my Achilles heels are always the same. One is not being enough— the fear of not being loved or accepted— or doing things in the right way so that I am enough. And the other one is not being in control. Being in control is something that has always made me feel safe, even when being in control meant I was actually making the situation worse.

Those two things are my Achilles heels that I constantly have to mindfully work past when I get into a period where I am caught in between the now and the not yet. That waiting feels like forever, and it feels like failure. Where I am now is trying to recognize, honor, and then move past the feeling of not enough, and the scary feeling of having a lack of control. This is a place I've been before. Yet, It's a place that I have never been as this version of me in. And it sucks. And it feels like I will never learn the lessons.

I do, and have, spent a lot of time trying to continually grow as a person and build my quiver of tools, my tool belts of ways to see the world, ways to see myself, ways to relate and move through the world in a better, more balanced and authentic way. Every iteration of myself is a stronger version. So this period that I'm going through right now, I have never been a stronger person than I am in this moment. I have never had more personal growth and development behind me. I have never been more authentic than I am today. Yet I still go through moments like this. Bleh.

One thing I've been thinking about as I'm moving through this void or sort of suspended animation is that I'm so grateful that I do have a few more tools to help me navigate it. Mindfulness and taking the time for self-care and for quiet and for rest? Those are tools that even a few years ago, I didn't have. Having those now is really helping me go through this period. It's certainly not a magic button. None of the tools that you will develop on your own journey are a magic bullet to save you or to insulate you from down periods. It's unrealistic to think that they are.

But I'm so grateful that I have built up the tools that I have because I feel like I have a much better perspective on what's happening than I would have at any other time. That mindfulness really helps. I think the other thing is that through exercising that muscle of being my authentic self, of being vulnerable and putting myself out there and making scary decisions that felt true to me to push myself forward, I have seen glimpses of what the fully manifested, fully realized, authentic me looks like and feels like. And because I've experienced that, I'm not willing to look away from it. Though – I admit I am kind of squinting at it right now.

While I'm in this period of hearing the negative voices and feeling the feelings, I know it will be ok because I've seen what's on the other side of it. So I'm willing to walk through this now. And I know that everything is temporary. This is temporary. (I keep chanting this, hoping it sticks) I know this, and I know this because I now have the skill and the presence to be able to look back and realistically assess where I've come from. For all of us, this is something that's really important. When you are in a period of feeling down or you're in between transformation stages, It's really easy to think that this is the end of the world. It definitely feels that way sometimes. I gaze with reminiscence at the shower I used to love to cry in.

It's really easy to think that that's it— this was the last bad decision— and now everything's over for me. But when you pause, and you can actually look back at the story of your life, what you actually see is that every time something hard came about, you got past it one way or the other, and you didn't die. You came out the other side, and you went on to do things that you never could have planned or imagined that you would or could do. That is another skill that I'm using right now to go through this period. And as I write that my thought is – yeah, but THIS time it's probably really true . . .

When those ego voices are so loud telling me that I don't know what I'm doing, I am a failure, everything and everyone and the universe is out to get me. This is it. I'm about to be homeless, or I'm about to have no friends, or I'm about to have no job, or whatever those voices are telling me. When I look back over the now almost 55 years of my life. And I see the various iterations of myself, and how even at my, what I'll say, at my dumbest, even at my least informed stages before I had done any personal development or growth, I still managed to stumble my way through hard time and move on to do better things.

I remember so many instances of that! We all have them. If you just look back and pay attention and see what you've really done— where time and time again— you do manage to get through it. But when you're in the middle of it, it feels like this is it. This is the last time, this is the last bad choice, bad break, bad decision, that this is not recoverable. But every single time it was. To have built that muscle to be able to have that perspective is something that's really helping me this time. Let me be honest, it does not stop me from having a crying jag for no reason, randomly on a Tuesday afternoon while I'm driving my car.

Nor does it stop me from eating some less than healthy comfort food as a way to numb and self soothe myself. I do all those things, just like any other human being. And also I get my butt up and make myself go to yoga, or go for a walk in the woods, or read a book that has nothing to do with business or personal development. It's just a really good novel— probably a romance, probably takes place on a beach. I do all the things that we all do. But what's different now is that I also understand what's happening, and I also understand that even though I hear the voices just as loudly as I ever have. I know that they're false.

I know that they're made up. I know this now in my core. Of course, the chattering is still there. Of course the fear is still there. Of course, the feeling down and wanting to beat myself up— those things are all still there. They don't disappear just because you've elevated to some level of personal development. But you have a better standing for being able to get outside of yourself and see them for what they are. They can be there, you can recognize them, and then you can move past them. My strategy the last couple weeks has been, feel my feelings, and then find at least one thing in that day that I can do.

That gives me a break from what's going on inside. That's self-care, self love. It puts a change in my routine that doesn't allow me to, you know, sit in this swirl of negativity. Just one thing. And if I continue to have the power to do one thing that is positive and moves me forward. It doesn't have to be 10. I'm, I'm not trying to, I'm not trying to, you know, be a world achiever. But if I have the power to do that one thing every day that moves me forward, even when I'm feeling my worst, Then I'm still in control of myself. I am still the one who is deciding that I'm moving through this, not falling into it.

And so that's what I wanted to share with you— that no matter how much work you do to develop yourself personally and to grow and to learn and to live as authentically as you know how, no matter how much effort and time you've put into that— you're still going to have those times when you question yourself. You're still going to have those times when you feel down and you feel afraid or you feel unsafe.

127

The difference is, every time you go through those, as you continue on your journey to grow and to become more authentic, you can stand in that. with more strength. You can stand in that with more perspective. And that's going to allow you to experience and move through those times. In a healthier way. In a more empowered way. And in a more empathetic way to yourself.

And I think that's, that's the best that we can all hope for, and it really is something that makes all the difference. Because I remember, you know, 5, 10 years ago it was so much more painful to go through these periods of time. And it was so much more damaging, I think, to my forward progress in fully expressing myself authentically. It was so much easier to retreat. It didn't mean I failed, but I certainly was setting myself back several steps from where I was trying to get to. And so what this time feels like is a pause.

So rather than becoming so fearful and so feeling out of control and feeling like such a failure, rather than allowing that to set me back months or years from my progress to where I envisioned my life to be— this feels like a pause. This feels like me standing still right where I am, and just allowing this to pass through me. While at the same time, having that strength to at least do that one little thing every day to move myself forward, at least emotionally.

So, I, I hope it's helpful for you to hear my personal experience and know that, you know, the idea, the, the goal, is not perfection— for any of us. The goal is to know ourselves, and the goal is to give ourselves the tools. To understand when we have those particularly vulnerable human moments. To get through them and realize that they're temporary and they don't have to be setbacks. They can just be pauses. Until we continue to move forward, being our authentic selves.

So yeah. I'm in the suck right now. And it's OK. And if you're there too, Or if you've been there. Or inevitably when you're there in the future. Just know that it's something we all go through, and it's OK. And while you're on this journey to learn about yourself and to live your life authentically, you also have built up tools. They're going to help you more easily get to the other side and get on with getting on. It's a given. So I hope that you think about that the next time you go through one of these periods. I know for me, I know this will pass. I know that I am making decisions and taking actions and resting when I need to.

And I am having feelings that are all authentically me, and I own all of them, and I know that they're leading me to the place that is my best self. And I also know that as much as I still try to envision what that path exactly looks like, I'm not going to know. And so for all I know, I'm going to look back on this in 5 years and kind of laugh that I was right where I needed to be all along because it took me to this next great thing. These are the kind of things I keep trying to tell myself as I go through this period of time in my life, and I hope that my experience gives you a little perspective on your own.

I think it's important to talk about it. I think it's important that we not hide from each other when we have those experiences, because that is something that is a major contributor to us feeling alone and disconnected and like we're the only ones. We clearly are not, but it's hard to be vulnerable, and it's hard to come out and admit mistakes or admit failure. Admitting confusion, particularly When you are someone who people look to for advice or support or love or any of those things that tend to make us feel like we have to be some perfect version of a human to deserve or have the right to be a person that someone else looks to, and that's completely ridiculous.

It is our fully flawed humanness that allows us to relate and connect. And it's that unvarnished experience that is so valuable when we are loving and supporting other people as well. Because we're not on a pedestal, we're not behind some shiny glittery wall away from other humans. We're right in the mix with everyone else, and it's the only way that we're going to get through it all is to be vulnerable and be open. And share our experiences and learn not only from our own experience, but the experiences that other people are having too.

A BRAVE Breath

"You can be unfinished and still be worthy of your own life."

WAYPOINT SIX — THE EXPANSION

"Where one woman living out loud becomes a ripple that changes everything."

The Expansion is the stage where your personal transformation ripples outward into the world. You've done the inner work. You've reclaimed yourself. You've integrated your new way of being. And now you're ready to expand— to share your story, your gifts, your presence with others. The Expansion is about contribution, connection, and collective transformation. You're no longer just living for yourself. You're living as part of a larger movement of women waking up, reclaiming themselves, and changing the world by changing themselves.

We Are All the Same

"It is in recognizing our sameness that we become free to be ourselves"

I went to a funeral yesterday. And I didn't mean to— I stumbled upon it. I was exploring the city of Granada in Nicaragua, wandering without my GPS for a while, letting myself get a little lost on purpose. In the distance, I saw what looked like a beautiful old church. And those of you who know me know this: I love old churches. So of course I walked toward it.

As I got closer, I noticed something in the median of the road— an ornate horse-drawn carriage. At first I thought it might be some kind of historic tourist attraction. But then I realized what it actually was: an old-fashioned hearse. Black wrought iron. Glass walls. Stunning in a way that made my stomach drop a little once I understood why it was there. I climbed the steps and crossed the threshold of the church, and immediately realized a service was already in progress.

So, I did the respectful thing: I put my phone away, stopped being a tourist, and slipped into the back pew. It would have been more awkward to turn around and leave at that point. It wasn't until a few moments later that I noticed the open casket at the front. I couldn't see inside it, but I could see it clearly enough to know this wasn't a Mass. This was a funeral.

And then I realized something else. Even though the priest was speaking Spanish— and even though I don't speak much Spanish – I could follow along. I was raised Catholic-*ish*. And the rhythm of the service... the framework... the gestures... the structure... it was familiar. Peace be with you. Passing of the plate. Communion. The prayers I've heard in English, in Italian, even Latin— different language, same bones.

And that's what struck me. It's the same everywhere.

Humans everywhere do the same things— in different ways— but with the same core needs underneath. We worship what matters to us.

We grieve. We celebrate. We cook food. We do laundry. We fall in love. We lose people. We make meaning. We try to belong. Life keeps happening, in every neighborhood, in every country, in every culture. And sitting there in that church— watching something both familiar and completely unfamiliar unfold at the same time— felt like a gift.

It reinforced something I already believe deep down: we get so convinced that *our* way is the way. That two plus two equals four is the only truth. But one plus three also equals four. So does four plus zero. So does 1.5 plus 2.5. There are so many ways to arrive at the same outcome . . .and we forget that.

So here's what I want you to consider the next time you start slipping into special snowflake syndrome— the belief that your pain is singular, your struggle is uniquely isolating, or your triumph is something no one else could possibly understand. We are all a human population. And at our core… we are far more alike than we are different. Not that our lives are interchangeable— but that our humanity is shared.

And that's what "we are all the same" means to me.

Because when one woman tells the truth about what she's carrying, something in another woman exhales. She feels human. She feels less alone. She realizes she was never meant to carry her life silently.

That is where belonging begins.

You just have to be real.

And you don't have to be extraordinary for it to matter.

It's medicine.

Because the truth is:
Your story isn't just yours.

She becomes a permission slip.

And when one woman chooses to live out loud— to tell the truth, to stop shrinking, to start becoming- she becomes a mirror for everyone around her.

Not that our lives are interchangeable— but that our humanity is shared.

That's what "we are all the same" means to me.

You were meant to be held.
You were meant to be mirrored.
You were meant to be met.

You were never meant to carry your life silently.
You were never meant to make it through heartbreak or reinvention without being witnessed.
You were never meant to keep performing your way into acceptance.

And the truth is, you were never meant to do this alone.

But strength without softness becomes a cage.

And this matters so much in midlife, because so many of us have spent decades being *capable*.
We've been the strong one.
The reliable one.
The one who holds it together.

That is where belonging begins.

The kind that says:
"I'm struggling."
"I'm grieving."
"I don't know what I'm doing."
"I'm tired of pretending."
"I want to be seen."

Not polished honesty.
Not "I'm fine now" honesty.
The real kind.

A BRAVE Breath

"You are not alone in what you feel. The moment you stop hiding your humanity is the moment connection becomes possible."

Happiness Does Not Exist (Out There)

"You won't find yourself by chasing — only by returning."

Happiness does not exist out there. Is that what it sounded like in your head when you read it? This is one of those moments where emphasis (or punctuation) matters. What I want you to hear is: **happiness does not exist...** *out there.*

I've been thinking about this because a recent Gallup World Poll came out, and one of its outputs is the World Happiness Index. A couple things really jumped out at me. First, the United States dropped in the global ranking— from the 15th happiest country down to 23rd. That felt significant. But the second thing was even more interesting: people over 60 reported higher well-being and happiness than younger adults. In fact, Americans over 60 ranked 10th in the world for happiness. Meanwhile, people under 30 reported a noticeable decline in well-being— and that seems to be a newer trend. And of course, I immediately went: *Wait... what?* Because younger people have their whole lives in front of them. What could be causing that kind of decline?

Now, to understand why this is so unusual, it helps to know what researchers call the U-curve. The U-curve shows that younger people typically report high happiness levels early in life... then well-being declines into its lowest point during midlife... and then rises again after age 60. And honestly, that makes sense. Kids don't carry the weight of adulthood. They play, imagine, belong, and get their needs met. They don't have mortgages, work stress, or complicated relationship dynamics. Childhood is messy, sure— but generally, children experience more joy. Then adulthood hits, and the complexity piles on. Responsibilities multiply. Our happiness erodes. And then— at some point— something shifts again. Maybe it's perspective. Maybe it's simplification. Maybe it's retirement. Maybe it's just finally deciding you're done proving yourself. But for many people, happiness rises again in later life. So, the U-curve checks out.

But here's the new part: That early "high happiness" phase— the beginning of the U— is now showing lower well-being than the older adults. That's what's different. And it made me wonder: what has changed so drastically for people under 30? I have to believe part of it is this constant overload of external input about what happiness is *supposed* to look like. Because younger people don't just have hopes and goals— they have access to a 24/7 fire hose of curated lives, manufactured perfection, and constant comparison. They're plugged into the world through their devices, and with that comes an endless stream of messaging:

- *This is what success looks like.*

- *This is what love should look like.*

- *This is what your body should look like.*

- *This is what happiness looks like.*

- *If you don't have it, you're doing it wrong.*

And if you're under 30, you're absorbing that at full volume— all day, every day. So it makes sense that well-being would decline. Because you're not just trying to build a life… you're trying to build a life while being told you're already behind.

Let's acknowledge the toll of that for a second. The emotional and mental exhaustion of being bombarded with: glamorized "perfect" lives on social media, marketing messages promising that the next gadget, trip, glow-up, or relationship will finally make you whole, this underlying cultural competition that says, *keep up or you've failed at life.* And we start to measure ourselves against all of it. How do we compare? How do we rank? How do we measure up? It becomes one more category we can fail at: *Happiness*.

And here's the cruel part: even when we get what we're chasing, the finish line disappears. You've seen this before. Maybe it's a promotion. A milestone. A relationship. A new house. A "dream" job. You work your ass off, convinced: *If I just get this one thing, then I'll finally feel happy.* And then you get it. You feel proud. Excited. Validated. Maybe even relieved. And then… what's the very next thought?

What's next?

Because happiness isn't a destination. It cannot be. There is always another rung. Another milestone. Another goalpost. Another "after that." And if your happiness is tied to external achievement, you will always find yourself chasing the next thing… and the next thing… and the next thing. That isn't happiness. That's a hamster wheel.

This is why happiness cannot be "out there."

The external world will always pull you into time travel: regret about what you didn't do in the past and anxiety about what you're supposed to do in the future. External validation makes you look backward and forward— but rarely *right here*. And that means your joy gets robbed by something you don't even have control over. Using the outside world to determine your happiness is a cruel joke you play on yourself. Because you can't win that game.

Instead, happiness is an inside job. Contentedness must come from inside you. It cannot be tied to a rule, a thing, a number, or somebody else's opinion about your life. Now, I can practically hear you rolling your eyes: *Okay, great. Here we go. Here comes the woo-woo. I need to meditate, journal, breathe, be present, blah blah blah…* I get it. And yes— those things *can* help. But I want to offer you something a little different.

I have a friend I love spending time with— he's done a lot of mindset work through martial arts, discipline, and resilience training. And one day he said something that landed so hard for me: The biggest reason people stay trapped in disappointment is because they haven't truly internalized the concept of **enough.** Because when you're chasing happiness out there, you're living in a cycle where: whatever you've been told will make you happy… is only the starting bid. From there, the ante is always upped. The goalpost always moves. There's always "one more thing."

So instead of only relying on mindset tools, you can approach this from a grounded perspective:

What does "enough" mean for you?

Not enough according to social media.
Not enough according to advertisers.
Not enough according to your mother's voice in your head.
Not enough based on what the world says your life should look like.

Enough for you. Because *enough* is where joy lives. Enough is where peace begins.

One practical tool for this came from a coach I worked with years ago— back when I was a toxic planner and spent a lot of time worrying about the future, obsessing over money, bracing for disaster, and basically assuming I was going to die. (You know. The usual.) She said: When you get spun up in "what's next," look down at your feet. Your feet are always with you. They're planted on the ground. They anchor you in the present moment. So step one: look at your feet. Step two: do a scan— physical, emotional, mental— of where you are right now.

Most of the time, if you're honest, you'll realize:

You have your health.
You've eaten.
You have shelter.
You have *something* that is supporting you.

138

You have people who care.
You are safe in this moment.

And in that moment, you have enough. Even with money— think about this: If you don't have a bill due in this exact second, and you don't need to spend money right now… then you technically have exactly enough money for *this moment*. It's a powerful reframe. Because instead of time traveling into anxiety, you come back to truth.

And speaking of time travel… There was a Netflix series called "The Mind Explained," and in the episode about memory, they talk about how your brain is constantly time traveling: to the past and to the future— imagining and remembering (often inaccurately) things you *think* you should be concerned about. It's exhausting. And it's also useless— because you can't do anything about the past, and the future isn't here yet.

So if control is what makes you feel safe? Control *this moment*. Be present here. Do a clear-eyed assessment of where you are and what you have— right now— without qualifiers. And allow yourself to realize:

You are okay right now.
You have enough right now.
You can feel contented right now.

We rob ourselves of joy when we let the monkey brain time travel on autopilot without our permission. So enjoy the bite of food. Enjoy the hug. Enjoy the ocean. Enjoy doing good work that matters to you. That is happiness. That is enough.

There is zero reason to delay happiness. Not until retirement. Not until the next promotion. Not until you lose ten pounds. Not until you make the next $1,000. Not until you get the next relationship or the next child or the next milestone.

There is no rule that says: *If I do this, then I can finally be happy.*

139

Or:

If I hadn't messed up in the past, that was my one shot at happiness, and now I missed it.

Let that land.

Because I genuinely believe that's the cycle most people are stuck in—especially now, in a world where we're constantly exposed to curated slivers of other people's lives and marketed versions of what happiness "should" look like. And when we're on autopilot, we can't help it. We immediately start ranking ourselves. And that steals our joy.

So, here's my challenge to you: **Look at your feet.** Where are you right now? What is enough? What can you enjoy in this moment— without letting it be ruined by something that happened in the past, or something that has a 99% chance of not even happening in the future? What can you connect to right now that gives you real happiness? Because I think that's the only way off the hamster wheel.

It takes practice— because we're not used to it. We're not used to being experts in our own lives. We get our standards, our "rules," and our validation from everyone else. And we dismiss the only person who truly knows us. But the only expert in you is you.

So don't worry, be happy— as they say. Where are your feet?

A BRAVE Breath

"Stop chasing what your soul is asking you to cultivate."

Curious About Curiosity

"Curiosity is the courage to stay open."

I'm curious about your thoughts on curiosity.

You may have heard me describe myself as a curious citizen of the world, and the word *curiosity* can mean a lot of things to a lot of people. In fact, many people consider curiosity to be a negative. Think of some of the old sayings we've all heard:

- Curiosity killed the cat.

- Ignorance is bliss.

- Don't ask questions you don't want to know the answers to.

- Mind your own business.

- What you don't know can't hurt you.

The overarching theme is this: if you don't know, you can remain safe. If you don't know, you can stay comfortable inside your current belief and identity system. And at its core, that idea—don't be the tall poppy, don't stand out, don't create waves—has been a survival mechanism for a lot of us. Maybe all the time. Maybe only in certain situations. So yes. I get it.

But curiosity is also one of the only ways we grow. We have to take in new information—both to pressure-test our identity and beliefs, and to stay willing to reevaluate and refresh how we see the world.

This has been on my mind because I recently came across a TEDx talk out of Bellevue, Washington by Julie Pham, a PhD and consultant in the Seattle area. Her talk is about curiosity as a practice, and I've watched it several times.

She says a lot of us define curiosity as the desire to learn. She adds that curiosity also includes **the effort** to learn. And she argues that expectations about what we *should* be learning often get in the way of what we *could* be learning.

That landed for me.

Because when it comes to belief systems, identity systems, and all the facades we wear to survive—to stay acceptable, to be included—there's always that list of *shoulds*. Do the shoulds, and you'll be safe. Do the shoulds, and you'll be included. Do the shoulds, and you'll be right. But those shoulds, as Julie describes it, get in the way of the coulds.

And if you think about the world we live in, there are infinite things we *could* be curious about… and probably an endless list of things we *should* be learning. That can make us feel like we don't have the bandwidth. Or it can make us feel overwhelmed by the sheer size of it all.

So, we stick to the "should" list like it's the vegetables we have to eat before we get dessert. And we don't allow our curiosity to move beyond those bounds—especially when we add in all the messaging that says curiosity makes you unsafe. That you'll fail. Be proven wrong. Feel embarrassed. Discover something uncomfortable. You know what I mean. All of those dynamics are in play when it comes to curiosity, openness, and vulnerability.

Julie goes on to explain that there's what we expect of a situation—our lives, our careers, our relationships—and then there's what we get. And between those two things is a gap. And it's that gap that prevents us from learning. It's the gap that freezes curiosity.

Think about any time you had a vision for how something would play out:

- a family vacation

- a career trajectory

142

- a birthday party you planned

- a new workout routine you swore you'd stick to

You had an idea of how it would go… and then reality happened. And what you got was different.

When we get stuck in that gap—between what we expected and what we got—feelings come up: anxiety, anger, shame, self-criticism. All the things we tend to do when life doesn't follow our script. I know this personally. As I've often admitted, I'm a recovering toxic planner. I like to know what's coming. I like details nailed down. I like a plan—usually with 1,000 steps—so I can remain in control of the universe… so everyone is safe, and I am safe.

And when those plans went sideways, it wasn't unusual for me to spin out, throw a tantrum, or have a strong emotional reaction. That reaction is often the signal: I'm stuck in the gap. I'm not learning. I'm not curious. So that's a red flag to notice: when there's a mismatch between what you planned and what you got—and your nervous system goes into revolt.

Another example where curiosity became important for me—as a practice, not a personality trait—came from something that *felt* like rejection.

I've traveled many places. I've learned a lot, discovered a lot, and documented plenty of it on social media. I've shared those experiences with friends and family. A couple years back, some friends were planning a once-in-a-lifetime dream trip to Italy to celebrate their anniversary. One stop was a place where I had spent a month—finding incredible hikes, out-of-the-way alleyways, amazing restaurants and shops. I was *so* excited to share what I'd learned.

So I waited.

And waited.

And waited.

Not a single question as they planned their trip. Then they left. They flew to Italy and posted things they discovered along the way. They reached the town I knew so well…and still nothing. Not a DM. Not a text. Not a WhatsApp. Not a call. And I was hurt.

I was frustrated—maybe even a little angry. I thought, *I have all this information. It feels kind of rude. Petty, even. Why wouldn't they ask?* Right? Have we all been there? And then—after I felt my feelings (because yes, feelings are allowed)—I remembered something.

One of the things I love most about travel is the satisfaction of finding my own way: the adventure and challenge of discovering things nobody told me about. So why did I feel entitled to their trip unfolding *my* way? The very thing that made travel exciting for me was exactly what they were doing: having their own experience, making their own discoveries, creating memories unique to *their* trip.

But when I was stuck in the gap—between what I expected and what I got—I couldn't be curious. I was frozen in discomfort, disappointment, and that irrational story that it was somehow about me. And I think that's one of the biggest things we do as humans: we take things personally. We assume we're at the center of everything—as if what's happening is because of us, or for us.

The reality is: everybody is living their own story.

It was such a useful reminder to come out the other side of those emotions and see the nuance: my friends were having the time of their lives because they're a lot like me. Of course they wanted their experience to be their own. And if I hadn't crossed that gap between expectation and reality, I would have missed that lesson completely.

To truly get curious—and break the pattern—you have to find a way to cross the gap. There are a couple ways to approach that.

First: recognize that when you're standing "over here," making your plans and setting your expectations, your view of "over there" is limited. Narrow. Incomplete. As Julie describes it, curiosity requires you to move closer—to see more clearly what's actually there.

A simple example is travel. People live differently. They speak differently, eat differently, commute differently, work differently, celebrate differently. If you stay in your bubble of what's familiar, it's unlikely your interactions will match your expectations—because you're observing from a distance, without enough context to understand the outcome.

Curiosity requires you to step outside the bubble. Maybe not fully immerse but at least dip a toe into the unfamiliar. Move closer. Expand your vantage point. Because you can't accurately assess something you're squinting at from "off yonder."

Second—and this one can feel even more uncomfortable—curiosity may require learning from someone you disagree with. That can feel triggering because our egos want us to be right. And we spend a lot of our lives—consciously or not—collecting evidence that proves we are right. We all do it. No judgment. Just reality. But that also shuts us down from new information. Sometimes the mere thought that we could learn something from someone we disagree with feels threatening enough to slam the door.

But here's the thing: listening does not equal surrender. Learning does not mean you must abandon your convictions. There is no rule that says that.

You might change your mind over time—because that's what evolving humans do. And there will also be beliefs you hold your whole life. Both can be true.

So instead of treating disagreement like a battleground, what if curiosity simply asks:

- What's their story?

- How did they come to believe that?

- What has it been like for them to live inside that worldview?

Not to convert them—or be converted—but to understand how other humans move through the world. Here's a simple illustration: 2 + 2 = 4. That's true. And also someone else might get to 4 through 1 + 3. Different math, same outcome. You can apply that to almost anything.

We want similar outcomes: happy families, meaningful work, health, belonging, success, peace. But there are a million different equations that get people there. And because we've lived one version, we start to believe it's the only version.

I remember traveling to "the end of the world." If you remember, 12/21/2012 was supposed to be the end of the Mayan calendar—so my family and some dear friends went to Mexico, to the center of Mayan culture, to experience the "end of the world." Our plan on the fateful day was to go to Chichén Itzá.

We took a tour bus, and our guide was incredible. As we drove through small villages, many people on the bus reacted the same way: with a privileged North American lens, those villages looked like poverty, dirt, sadness—"the worst of the worst." I had my own version of that reaction too. This was many years ago, and I remember thinking, *Wow… what a terrible way to live.*

And our guide gently shifted our perspective. He invited us to look closer. He pointed out tightly knit community. Pride. Multigenerational households. Children playing and inventing games with what they had. People who—at their core—wanted the same things we do: to belong, to love, to be useful. And when you looked again, you could see it: they were getting to the same "answer" we were… with different math.

That moment stayed with me. It taught me why approaching people, cultures, and mindsets with empathy and openness matters—not because you're swaying in the wind, but because it gives you permission. When you see that other people get to the outcome in different ways, it becomes less risky for you to find what works for *you*,

146

especially when the way you've been conditioned to live no longer feels comfortable.

And on the flip side: it reminds you that people who are different from you are also doing what works for them. That kind of empathy is how we create less conflict, less misunderstanding, and more connection. It's also how we become true curious citizens of the world: moving through our towns, societies, and cultures—and into other cultures—without immediately trying to correct or criticize. First: curiosity. First: empathy. First: appreciation.

This is what curiosity can do for you. And I think the big takeaway about curiosity as a practice is to make it personal. On the journey to reclaim our authentic identities, we must be curious:

- Why have I held so tightly to this belief or story?

- Why does that trigger me?

- Why does this feel unsafe?

- Why do I react like this when the universe does what the universe does?

If we can start from curiosity rather than condemnation—like Ted Lasso says, *be curious, not judgmental*—we give ourselves a deeper insight into how we tick. When we keep asking questions with open-ended answers, we stay in conversation with ourselves. We allow our spirit—our soul—to be in conversation with our ego, even though our ego rarely wants to share the mic.

Through curiosity, empathy, and kindness, we start to understand why we believe what we believe. And for the beliefs we *can't* explain—maybe that's the place to start. Maybe that's the doorway to re-curating something truer.

Curiosity is a powerful tool. And being willing to ask questions—even at the risk of failing, sounding dumb, or hearing something you didn't want to hear—is how you move closer. It's how you close the gap between what you expect and what you get. That's where everything starts: inside you.

And when that curiosity expands outward—into how you move through the world—it becomes even more powerful. We show up with questions instead of verdicts. We seek to understand before deciding something is wrong. We inch closer. We broaden our view.

And because we can see more, we feel more confident. Braver. Safer.

The unknown is what creates discomfort. So, the more we understand, the safer we feel. And the safer we feel, the more willing we become to explore and question what we "know"—which we should be doing our entire lives. Because stuff changes. New information. Natural evolution. Nothing in the universe is perfectly rigid. If we aren't flexible enough to move with it, we get left behind—and we never quite find that place where we truly feel like ourselves.

A BRAVE Breath

"Stay open. Move closer. Stay curious."

Connection and Community

"We don't heal alone— we heal in witness."

I had been going through the suck— going through another period of being *caught between the now and the not yet.* That discomfort and chaos that tends to show up right before the next level of evolution or transformation. And it gave me an opportunity to pause and think about the tools I've developed over the years to help me navigate these cycles. One that keeps rising to the top is community and connection.

You might be surprised by how pervasive loneliness is. In our culture, it's an unspoken epidemic of sorts. But I want to talk more deeply about the connection between loneliness and community— because it's been a theme showing up everywhere in my life. Connection and community are things I place a lot of value and emphasis on. The tagline for my business, *She Lives Out Loud,* is: "connection, community, aliveness." So it's definitely a cornerstone of who I am.

And it's also a departure from how I lived for a long time— certainly over the last several years of my adult life. I had a force field of sorts… a coat of armor around me as I navigated living in a skin I didn't fit in, living in an inauthentic way. And the only way to keep my secret, so to speak, was to not allow anyone to get beyond the surface I was willing to show. So inside, I was isolated— even while the outside version of me looked vivacious and well-connected. Lately I've been thinking a lot about this concept of community… a tribe… deep connections with other humans— and why it can feel so hard.

There's a contradiction we live with. We prize individualism. We celebrate being different. And yet, we also talk constantly about finding your tribe— people who are *just like you.* It's the paradox of wanting belonging, while also needing to stay open to other ways of thinking and living. Being open to the unfamiliar— through travel, learning, observing, or whatever doorway you walk through to get there.

Recently, I attended adult summer camp for people trying to find their "special sauce" balance between time, money, and location freedom. It was such an incredible gathering of people trying not only to find their tribe… but to do it in their own way. One of the keynotes gave a talk about finding her path while also being a fugitive from the FBI. Intriguing, right? But one of the things she talked about was this idea that we need both: we need to put ourselves in situations where we get out of our own Kool-Aid— out of our own way of thinking— and become open to other truths that are just as real, just as correct, and just as authentic as ours. And at the same time, we need to find the tribe of people who *get it*. Who get us. Who are like us in the ways that matter. And there *is* a way to do both.

Life is paradox everywhere you look. So part of growth is learning how to hold paradox without needing to fix it. Our brains want one answer: right or wrong, hot or cold, kind or mean. But life rarely gives us those clean lines. We are wired to want and crave belonging— to be part of something bigger. In the beginning of time, it was for survival. Now, it's for connection and acceptance. And yet, so many of us feel disconnected from deep connection. So why does it feel so hard to feel understood or supported by the communities and tribes that could be the key to us becoming our strongest, most authentic selves?

Part of it is the cultural emphasis on individualism. We celebrate the standout person— the one who goes their own way— and we give them the blue ribbon. But then there's the other side: when they stand out *too much,* when their individuality starts to make us uncomfortable, that's when we reel them back in. That's when we tear them down. So yes— there's a paradox: be an individual… but don't be *so* much of an individual that you threaten me and how I feel about myself. I think we see that everywhere— especially online.

150

We also live in a world where so much is curated. It's frowned upon to show your warts. There's pressure to hide the parts that aren't polished— especially during seasons when things aren't going the way we want... or the way we want people to believe. So, we hide. Because we fear rejection. We fear not belonging. We fear being on the outside. And hiding can feel like self-preservation. But when you look at all the factors that make deep connection hard, one piece is simple: many of us were never taught the tools for how to navigate shame, embarrassment, and fear. And you can't learn the tools *without* walking through those feelings. You have to feel the discomfort to get the lesson.

At no time in my past was I as proactive about seeking and nurturing deep vulnerable connections as I've been these last several months. And I do have a tribe around me now— people who understand me. What's interesting is that my tribe is made up of people who, while we share a few key areas of alignment, are wildly different from each other. And that, to me, is the strongest kind of tribe: one that isn't made of carbon copies. Because when your foundation people aren't identical to you, you get something stronger than an echo chamber. You get support. You get perspective. You get empowerment. You get to be seen and heard and celebrated by people who are different from you— and that is transformational.

I'm so grateful to be at a point in my life where I'm willing to take those risks, and I think it's because I've seen both sides of this coin. I've seen what happens when I protect myself— when I hide my challenges and mistakes in the name of being acceptable and relatable. And then I've experienced what happens when I do the counterintuitive thing: when I get vulnerable. When I let myself be seen.

And here's what I learned: Everything I did to "stay safe"— everything I did that came from fear, shame, or embarrassment— didn't protect me. It cut me off. It cut me off from the support I needed. It kept me in a cycle of keeping up appearances. It kept me from fully expressing who I am. But when I allowed myself to be seen— in all my imperfect glory— that's when I found the launching pad to truly be who I am.

To exhale. To experience joy and abundance in a world where I used to live holding my breath… clenching my abs… waiting for the next gut punch. That's what I'm realizing: if you want deep human connection, you have to step past fear. Somebody once said, *just past the fear lies the freedom.* And I think that's exactly what we're talking about here.

We tend to make fear important. We treat it as special. We almost befriend it. We let it take up all the space it wants in our lives. But what if we made fear… uninteresting? What if we treated it like any other obstacle we face in daily life— and just walked right past it? Because that's where freedom lives.

And I'll be honest: I'm a mess— a quivering, fearful mess— every time I reach out vulnerably. Every time I ask for help. Every time I admit a mistake. Every time I ask for a hug or a kind word. Every time I initiate a deep conversation with someone who matters. I'm admitting it. And also: every single time I do it, I'm grateful on the other side. Because what I receive— and what it feeds in me— is immeasurable.

I've found myself working that muscle even more recently. At camp, I didn't go to build my business, or to "achieve" something the way I might have last year. This time my intention was simple: connection. And I got it. The conversations. The real talks. The moments where I admitted my struggles. The moments where I listened—truly listened—to someone else's pain and someone else's joy. It was transformational.

And now, being back home— continuing to reach out to my tribe, sharing what I'm feeling, celebrating their wins, supporting them through their challenges— I'm realizing something: It becomes almost addicting. Not in a toxic way— but in a soul-nourishing way. Because once you get past the shaking and nervousness of vulnerability, what's on the other side is so joyful… and so real… and you realize how much your spirit has been craving it.

That said, I don't want to become so comfortable inside my tribes that I forget the paradox: stay open to the new. So, I've been making myself say yes to coffee with someone new— even when I'm internally grumbling about it. I've been making myself go on the first date. Try the new class. Meet people who are doing something I don't know how to do, where I might feel dumb. And what I'm finding is that I feel more joy than I've felt in a long time. Joy about the freedom I have in my life. Joy about the possibilities ahead of me— always ahead of me. And I'm confirming, again, that everything is paradox.

I'm moving through a challenging period where I question every adult decision I've ever made… and also, I have never been more joyful about what's in my life right now, and what's still unfolding. And I think that's the biggest lesson: the more you practice it, the more you can become comfortable— and even grateful— for the paradox that shows up everywhere.

Underneath all of this is one truth: You have to be willing to move through fear— and through the shame or embarrassment of being seen— because that is the only way your people can recognize you. The longer we hide behind our facades, thinking we're creating safety for ourselves, the harder we make it for the people who are meant to see us— to celebrate us, support us, love us. We make ourselves harder to find. And that is the paradox. To build real safety, you have to release your grip on the fake safety. You have to loosen the armor. You have to let the people who are meant for you see what's real. They have to be able to see through the smokescreen.

So remember this:

Just past the fear lies the freedom.

Let that give you the glimmer of courage to take the very next step—to be vulnerable, to be open, and to allow the right people to find you.

A BRAVE Breath

"The moment you tell the truth, you make it safe for others to exhale."

The Loneliness Factor

"Loneliness isn't proof you're broken— it's proof you're meant for connection."

How many of you have felt alone while spending time by yourself? What about in a room full of people you *don't* know? What about in a room full of people you *do* know? Have you ever felt lonely in a relationship— as a parent, a child, a partner, a boss, a friend, an employee, a leader? Have you felt lonely when everything is going wrong? Have you felt lonely when everything is going right?

Our mental and physical health is directly tied to our level of connectedness. And according to some studies, up to 60% of us feel lonely on a regular basis.

I want to link that to something we've talked about before: **we hide from each other.** We create this chasm between where we really are… and where we want people to *think* we are. And we live in that hiding space in between— because we're afraid that if we're found out, we'll be rejected… and lonely anyway. So, it almost feels like a no-win, right? We're wired to need belonging— emotional and physical safety. This is a big reason we create facades: a version of ourselves we believe will be acceptable… granted the privilege of being protected, being safe, being loved.

But unfortunately, every layer we put over our unvarnished, authentic selves widens the gap. And the loneliness grows. Loneliness can be externally driven or internally driven. But either way, when it's left unattended, it can have devastating effects.

There's an interview with Laurie Santos, a cognitive science and psychology professor at Yale. She teaches a class called *Psychology and the Good Life*— one of the most popular courses on campus— and it eventually led her to create a podcast called *The Happiness Lab*. She cites surveys suggesting up to 60% of people in the U.S. report feeling lonely regularly. Sixty percent. That's a higher percentage than people dealing with obesity or diabetes. And those numbers have been rising steadily since the 1970s.

Now, I don't think we can make a knee-jerk reaction and blame this solely on cell phones or social media. But we *do* have more distractions. We have less time— or at least less *available* time— to create meaningful human connection. After a hard day, we zone out to Netflix. We bring work home. We scroll social media or the news. We stack books on our nightstand that we "should" be reading. We squeeze soccer games, fundraisers, errands, and chores into our non-working hours— often just to keep up with that made-up idea of the "successful life." So, whether we blame screen time or not, the truth is: there are more things pulling at us than ever. And the more distracted we become— and the more we hide behind masks— the more isolated we feel.

And this isn't just emotional. Loneliness impacts our health. It's been linked to increased risk for dementia, heart disease, and stroke. It affects longevity. And the health impact of chronic loneliness has been compared to smoking 15 cigarettes a day in terms of overall harm to well-being. Think about that. You could be doing yoga, meditating, eating clean, walking in fresh air every day... and if you're trapped in persistent isolation, your body pays a price that serious.

Another survey from June 2023 reported that more than a third of U.S. adults say they feel alone or don't interact with others at least once a week— and 41% say lack of friends or community is the primary driver of their loneliness. And what's especially striking: younger adults (Gen Z and younger millennials) report feeling the most alone, while boomers report feeling the least alone. It isn't a massive gap— but it's meaningful. And higher-income Americans reported more loneliness than lower-income Americans. What we're watching unfold is a world that's becoming more complex— and more comparative. With digital connectedness, we have more ways to measure ourselves artificially, more ways to feel like we're behind, and more ways to believe we're the only ones struggling. So as younger people come of age in this environment, it makes sense they're feeling the brunt of the isolation more intensely than older generations who lived more of their lives in a simpler world. And while I think we all experience loneliness at different seasons, it's important to acknowledge: as our world becomes more digitally connected and more complex, we have to help younger people navigate this.

Now, yes— digital media plays a role. Some studies suggest we spend about 50% of our time digitally connected to something. For Gen Z, that number is higher— and for older adults, lower— but even the low end is still a lot of time spent online: scrolling, comparing, judging ourselves, and not creating the kinds of real connection that actually regulate the nervous system. Which brings me to this: the human need for community is not new.

In Japan, the ancient concept of Ikigai includes belonging and community as a key component of a balanced, meaningful life. (Side note: Ikigai has been heavily "corporatized" lately into a purpose-as-career map— and that's a pretty incomplete, sometimes irresponsible interpretation of a much more holistic concept.) My point is: if you're reading this, you've likely experienced loneliness or isolation. For many of us, it's regular— if not constant. And that becomes part of the messy soup of a self-imposed prison we build as we try to live "successfully" and come out the other side somewhat unscathed.

But I want to make one distinction really clear: Being alone does not automatically mean being lonely. I enjoy alone time. I travel alone. I live alone. I do a lot on my own— and I genuinely like it. When I experience loneliness, it isn't because I'm physically by myself. It's because I don't feel connected. Sometimes I can feel connected just people-watching in a park. So, it isn't about having "my people" in the room. It's about the feeling of *being unseen*: nobody gets me, nobody understands me, nobody to share the moment with, nobody to bounce the thought off of. So yes— being alone can be nourishing. Loneliness is different.

And yet... we keep feeding loneliness when we hide. We build a version of ourselves designed for acceptance. And then we wonder why we feel empty. We long for connection, for recognition, for authenticity— but we're afraid to show the very parts of ourselves we want to be loved for. So we sit inside this paradox:

We want to be seen. But we fear being seen. We want belonging. But we avoid the risk required to belong.

And the result is a vicious cycle where we can't fully experience joy, abundance, or peace. One of the hardest parts of dropping the facades— of living unapologetically— is the fear of being "the other." Not belonging. Being misunderstood. Being lonely. Our egos— as loud and obnoxious as they are— are trying to keep us safe. But here's the twist: when that safety mechanism kicks in, we often do the very things that move us *farther* from connection. Farther from community. Farther from ourselves. Another paradox. Maybe that's one of the themes of being human: conflicting things can both be true. And it doesn't always make sense. And that's okay.

So, if loneliness is one of the biggest forces that sabotages an authentic life... what do we do? You know what I'm going to say: You find the glimmer of bravery inside yourself... and you take one small step. One vulnerable step toward connection. And no, community is not always a bed of roses. It requires adjustment. It requires participation. It requires being willing to both give and receive— and that can feel scary. It can feel like effort. It can feel like a bother. So we opt out. But the first vulnerable step— letting someone see one real piece of you—

is what opens the door to the kind of community we're all craving. Not a group of people who agree with you on everything. (We're not building a mono-bot echo chamber.) We're talking about finding your people: the ones who get you, celebrate you, and make room for your complexity— your similarities and your differences. And there is simply no way that can happen if nobody knows who you are.

I know some of you are thinking, *Well… crap. If I put my real self out there, I'm just hanging off a cliff.* Yeah. It can feel like that. But logically? It's the only way. Your people can't recognize what they never get to see. And if you keep hiding it… they're not seeing it. For me, the craving for community has been lifelong. I've found it in pockets. I've also thought I found it— and later realized I was just playing a role: caretaker, hero, leader, worshiper, follower. At the time, I didn't know I was doing it. I only saw it in hindsight. And just recently, I experienced something that reminded me— again— how powerful community can be when vulnerability is allowed.

I went to a retreat in Mexico designed for deep personal work through all kinds of modalities: breathwork, meditation, "radical relating," ice plunges, sweat lodges— the whole toolkit for peeling back layers you didn't even realize were there. Now, I'm not saying everyone needs to go dive into the deep end like I did. But it's a good example of what I mean. Over the course of that week with a group of really special, like-minded people, we practiced vulnerability. We chipped away at the untruths— the protected stories— the armor we've carried for years, sometimes our whole lives. And what was interesting: there was no "corporate agenda." No neat schedule. Half the time we didn't know what we were doing next hour, let alone tomorrow. Which, for a recovering toxic planner like myself, was… a spiritual intervention. It forced presence. It forced surrender. It blocked me from manufacturing a "desired outcome" and then building a five-year plan around it. And it made room for what I actually needed.

Here's what surprised me: The most transformational thing I received from that retreat wasn't a big dramatic breakthrough. It was connection. community. belonging. I spent a week— sometimes painfully— peeling back layers and being more vulnerable than I've ever been. And yes: it's terrifying. The knots in your stomach. The urge to bolt. The moment where you wonder if you're about to be rejected for telling the truth. But slowly, as safety built, and the walls came down, I allowed people— many of whom began as strangers— to see the beginnings of who I really am. And what I found was acceptance. Understanding. Celebration. It was magic. I wouldn't trade that experience for anything.

There was also an altar-like space in the center of the room— a symbolic place where we brought items representing what we wanted to release… and something we wanted to carry back with us, infused with the energy of the collective. A lot of people— myself included— brought items representing people and situations we were finally ready to let go of… because they weren't in alignment with our truth. It's like renovating a home: you have to clear what's taking up space so you can build what's next. Letting go of those relationships created room for what I actually needed: true connection and community. And when I say subtle, I don't mean small. It was one of the most powerful experiences of being seen I've ever had— and the ripple effects began immediately: abundance, friendship, forward movement in my work and my life. It was like clearing leaves out of a gutter. Like breaking a dam. When you experience what it feels like to be seen— and then plugged into where you belong— life starts flowing differently. You have to feel it to understand it.

Now, obviously, not everyone can take a week off to go do a retreat. But there are other ways. Little steps. Low-stakes vulnerability. Testing the waters. Making space in your life— not just for yourself, but for the community that wants to support you. That does require vulnerability. So, here's the question: What are the small ways you can practice being seen… while still feeling relatively safe?

Because if you feel 100% safe and 100% protected all the time, you already know what that usually means: You're shut down. You're armored. You're staying exactly where the old system wants you.

And that system? It will happily keep you lonely— as long as you stay hidden.

A BRAVE Breath

"Loneliness is a signal— not a sentence."

The Spark

There's a moment when a woman knows.

She can't explain it — *but she feels it.*

It's not dramatic— but it's undeniable.

A quiet tremor under the surface,

a whisper that says,

This isn't who I came here to be.

She's done playing small.

Done following the rules that dim her light.

The world told her to stay quiet — *but her soul's not having it anymore.*

So she begins.

One breath, one truth, one brave choice at a time.

And as she rises, others see her.

They remember something they, too, had forgotten.

One becomes two.

Two become hundreds.

Hundreds become a movement.

Women living fully, fiercely, freely — not to prove their worth,

but because they finally know it.

This is not rebellion.

This is remembrance.

This is what happens when women live out loud.

About the Author

PHOTO BY SANDRA COSTELLO

Sharon Welch is a transformational speaker, coach, and aliveness activist devoted to helping women in midlife rediscover who they are beneath the layers of expectation, responsibility, and fear. After decades as a community builder, entrepreneur, corporate strategist and leader, Sharon experienced a series of "lifequakes" that dismantled the façade of success and catalyzed a profound personal awakening. Today, she guides women through that same journey of reclamation—helping them re-curate outdated beliefs, reconnect with their truth, stop performing and start becoming—and to rebuild lives that feel aligned, abundant, and unapologetically alive.

As the founder of **She Lives Out Loud**, Sharon creates spaces—on stage, in retreats, and within intimate communities—where women can drop their masks, speak their truths, and remember their power. Her story-driven keynotes and workshops blend insight, vulnerability, and humor, inviting audiences to move from breakdown to breakthrough and from façade to freedom.

Sharon brings a rare combination of strategic clarity and soulful presence to her work. Whether she's guiding a coaching client, leading a retreat circle, or speaking to hundreds of women ready for change, Sharon's message is always the same: you are not broken, you are becoming.

In her downtime, Sharon is probably near the water - likely reading, napping, travelling, or sharing meals, hugs, and belly laughs with her loved ones. Her son Parker is her proudest and most cherished creation.

Facebook: /shelivesoutloud   Instagram: @shelivesoutloudnow